THE BEST SEAT IN
THE HOUSE

THE BEST SEAT IN THE HOUSE

Stories from the NHL—Inside the Room, on the Ice…and on the Bench

Jamie McLennan
and Ian Mendes

John Wiley & Sons Canada, Ltd.

Library and Archives Canada Cataloguing in Publication Data

McLennan, Jamie, 1971-
    The best seat in the house : stories from the NHL—inside the room, on the ice...and on the bench / Jamie McLennan with Ian Mendes.

Includes index.
Issued also in electronic formats.
ISBN 978-1-118-30253-8

    1. McLennan, Jamie, 1971-.   2. Hockey goalkeepers—Canada—Biography.
3. Hockey players—Canada—Biography.   I.   Mendes, Ian, 1976- II.   Title.

GV848.5.M25A3 2012   796.962092   C2012-902844-4

ISBN 978–1–118–30481–5 (eBk); 978–1–118–30482–2 (eBk);
978–1–118–30483–9 (eBk)

Production Credits
Cover design: Adrian So
Cover photo credits:
    Front cover: Ian Tomlinson/Getty Images
    Back cover: Jamie McLennan photo: Geoff George Photography
              Ian Mendes photo: Sonia Mendes
Interior text design: Thomson Digital
Typesetter: Thomson Digital
Printer: Courier Corporation

John Wiley & Sons Canada, Ltd.
6045 Freemont Blvd.
Mississauga, Ontario
L5R 4J3

Printed in the United States

    2 3 4 5 COU 16 15 14 13 12

To my mom, Darlene, and dad, Stuart, brothers Darin and David and their respective wives and kids, thank you for always being there through the ups and downs of this ride. Lastly, but mostly, to my loves Steph and Bumbo, for making me happy and completing my life, thank you.
Mace, you are gone but never forgotten.
Merrily, merrily. . . . Life is but a dream.
Jamie

My writing career is a perfect blend of my mother's love for education and my father's passion for sports. To my mom, Phoebe, and my dad, Ashley, thank you for laying the foundation in my life. To my wife Sonia, your continued love and support allow me to live the dream of being both a father and a sports journalist. You will always be the best thing in my life.
Ian

Contents

Foreword
By Jarome Iginla

I could suggest a few other titles for Jamie's book but *The Best Seat in the House* certainly suits this guy's career. Miikka Kiprusoff believes he should have called it "The Guy Who Slashed Franzen." That came from Jamie's final game in the NHL. Six teams over 11 seasons and the most attention he received was in his final game, when he two-handed Johan Franzen and was suspended for five games. He served one and then retired. Yup, what a way to go out! Seriously though, that one incident speaks to his dedication and loyalty to his team in his role as a backup to Kipper in Calgary.

I won't ruin the rest of the story for you; besides laughing your butt off, you'll understand what I mean. Whether appearing in one of his 254 NHL games or taking the last seat at the end of the bench, Noodles played a very valuable role on every team he played with. If you look up the definition of "team guy" you'll find Jamie's picture. Actually, there are several words that also have his picture by them but might still get him in trouble if I reveal them. Nobody was ever better in the room then Jamie (maybe he should have stayed in the room). Through a great sense of humor, relentless pranks, constant chatter and chirping and a true "feel" for what the team needed in every situation, Noodles will always be remembered as a great teammate. He remains one of my closest friends and I cherish the time we find to spend together. I hope you enjoy reading his book as much as I did. Only he could get away with telling these stories.

Jarome Iginla

Foreword
By Roberto Luongo

Noodles was one of the friendliest, most down to earth, funniest teammates I've had the privilege to play with in my entire NHL career. From the moment I met him he made me feel at ease and I felt that he was very approachable. To this day we are still very good friends and keep in touch on a regular basis.

In the short period of time that we played together I learned a lot from him by the way he handles himself on and off the ice. He always looked like he was having fun at the rink and I think that is a major factor in being a great teammate. The fact that he has a huge heart and really cares about the game and his teammates so much is what makes him the most popular guy in the dressing room every year! His sense of humor is uncanny as everyone could tell in that video that we made for TSN. Here's to great success with this book!

Roberto Luongo

Acknowledgments

Ian and I would like to thank the many people who helped us complete *The Best Seat in the House*. First of all, to our literary agent, Brian Wood, for bringing us together to work on this project. A huge thanks as well to Karen Milner, Elizabeth McCurdy and the editorial and production teams at Wiley, for helping us polish the manuscript. We would also like to thank Sportsnet and TSN for their support and professionalism during this process. We would like to acknowledge the significant contribution from both Jarome Iginla and Roberto Luongo in writing the forwards for this book. Also, we would like to thank the following people for allowing us to share some unique stories: Chris Pronger, Miikka Kirpusoff, Darryl Sutter, Chad Kroeger, Grant Fuhr, Ron Hextall, Rhett Warrener, Jimmy Roberts, Billy Smith, Wendel Clark and many other teammates who were a part of this fun behind-the-scenes look. I would also like to thank the many teammates and organizations that I played for and with over the years and who always had my back and made this journey so enjoyable.

To my lifelong friends: Degs, Prongs, Moby, Yoely, Larue, Senny, Lums, Struds, Nasher, Holly, Iggy, Hanlon, Billy R, Leather, Foster, Bobo, Young Joseph, Jammer, Robyn, Rhettro, Kipper, Joshua Morrow, Louie, Marty the one man party, Greenie, Dion, Lombo, Ference, Chuck K, Commie, Chad, Mike, Ryan, Daniel, Chief and Brad (Nickelback), Tyler, Dean, Dave and Joe (Theory), and to Tanya and the boys and anyone else I have forgotten to include on this list, you guys have made me what I am today and I can never thank you enough.

And of course, we would like to point out that some of the names in this book were changed to protect the innocent and not-so-innocent.

Preface

When you reach your 40th birthday, it seems like a natural time to pause and reflect on life up to that point. I hit that milestone in the summer of 2011 and spent a good deal of time looking in my personal rearview mirror.

I sometimes laugh to myself because I considered myself the Forrest Gump of the National Hockey League: I always felt like I was in the background of a lot of memorable moments. When I got called up to the NHL as a rookie, I ended up voting to go on a players' strike just 24 hours into my career. I always seemed to be in the right place at the right time—or the wrong place, depending on how you look at it.

Nobody is likely to remember this, but I was actually Mark Messier's teammate with the Rangers when he played his final game in the National Hockey League. I was also there the night Mario Lemieux scored his 500th career NHL goal—but thankfully it was Tommy Soderstrom who was in net against the Penguins for that game. When Al Arbour reached a couple of major coaching milestones in his final season with the New York Islanders, Yours Truly was just a few feet down from him on the bench.

I often found myself on the end of the bench because I was teammates with some of the best goaltenders of my generation. There is no shame in playing second fiddle to the likes of Grant Fuhr, Ron Hextall, Roberto Luongo and Miikka Kiprusoff—but there are a lot of stories to tell. That's how we came up with the title for this book, *The Best Seat in the House*.

When you're the backup goaltender, a big part of your job is to make sure you are a good teammate inside the dressing room. In these pages, I want to allow the reader to peek inside a NHL dressing room and experience what the camaraderie is like behind closed doors. I'll take you to team parties where we were able to really enjoy ourselves—in an era before Twitter and phone cameras got so many star athletes in trouble. Foolishly, I once (temporarily) borrowed a taxicab in Montreal, but nobody was the wiser. Some nights guys used to go to the bar wearing nothing but underwear. Those things could never happen today without somebody having the grainy footage up on YouTube within a few hours.

One of the great perks of being a pro athlete is getting to hang with celebrities from other walks of life. I've been lucky to become good friends with Chad and Mike Kroeger and the rest of the band Nickelback. I even had a chance to meet one of my idols, Gene Simmons—but after the encounter I stopped being a KISS fan and took their logo off my goalie mask. I've had drinks with Wayne Gretzky and Mark McGwire and even accidentally called Lady Gaga a troll to her face.

Of course life as a professional hockey player wasn't always perfect. During my stops in Worcester, Salt Lake City and Richmond, I was not rubbing elbows with celebrities and flying on charter airplanes—and rightly so. My career in Russia only lasted a few weeks after somebody pulled a gun on our team bus. And I also had a near-death experience with meningitis that nearly cost me my career—and my life.

I'm not sure what the next 20 years hold in store for me. Since retiring from the game, I've worked in coaching and now broadcasting. I'm committed to getting better—whatever I end up doing long-term—but I know one thing for certain: I'm going to have a hard time matching the excitement level from the past 20 years.

1

The Early Years

I remember being 4 years old and playing organized hockey for the first time. It would be the equivalent of what they call Timbits Hockey today, but this was well before Tim Hortons had taken a stranglehold on naming everything in this country. Four-year-olds are small, so we were able to play three hockey games simultaneously on a single sheet of ice.

At first, I enjoyed the thrill of playing as a forward and scoring goals against the opposition. When I was 5 years old, we started to rotate goalies. At that stage in life, no child wants to be a goalie. Who in his right mind would want to be woken up at 5 a.m., be strapped into heavy equipment and then stand in a stationary position while all his friends are skating around and having fun? Most young teams simply rotate the job of goalie after every game so that everyone can share in the misery.

But for some reason, I immediately fell in love with the position. When you're playing goal at the age of 5 or 6, it's a pretty charmed life. The opposition players have no set plays, since most of them are still struggling with basic coordination on the ice. And when they have the puck in the slot, you know they can't beat you high glove side. Nobody could raise the puck off the ice at that point, which means I could've perfected the paddle-down style of goaltending before my seventh birthday.

Instead, like every young goalie back then, I was obsessed with perfecting the two-pad stack and the poke-check, and making the skate save—the technical moves that dominated the position in the pros at the time. Fast forward about 25 years, near the end of my NHL career, when I made a skate save one night in Los Angeles. It prompted the boys on the Flames bench to go crazy. Robyn Regehr even skated by me and yelled out, "Skate save—old-time hockey!"

I was a goalie from that point on and I think it gave me a significant edge growing up. By the time I was 10 years old, I was so used to wearing goalie equipment that everything came a bit more naturally to me than for some players who made the switch to goal later on.

The best time of year for me was always in September, when the shipment of new gear for the league would arrive. My dad would take me down to Akinsdale Arena in St. Albert and they would have all the goalie equipment strewn about in a little crawl space. The room was dark, dingy and poorly lit, yet it was the most magical place for a young goalie.

It was so exciting because you got to pick the pads, glove and blocker you were going to wear for the next six or seven months. I always wanted to get the brand-new stuff, but you had to make sure everything fit properly. There was no sense in looking super stylish, only to find out your pads were three sizes too big when you tried to play a game.

Just playing a game was sometimes an adventure in minor hockey. I distinctly remember driving with my dad for a game one night to a rink called Fultonvale, which is in a part of Edmonton that's now called Strathcona. We set out in our wood-paneled station wagon in search of the Fultonvale Arena. We always left for games with plenty of time to spare, because I had to get to the rink early with all my goalie gear.

But on this particular night, my dad just could not find the rink. In a northern Alberta winter, darkness comes in the late afternoon, so we were driving around in the pitch black looking for this arena. As we kept fumbling around in the dark looking for this elusive arena, I realized I wasn't going to make the game on time. It's usually okay if your second-line left winger shows up late, but when the goalie is lost five minutes before puck-drop, that's a bit of a problem.

My dad instructed me to get into the back seat and start putting on my equipment. I put on my pads, chest protector and even my skates, while he—visibly frustrated—popped in to a gas station to get directions. My dad is usually a pretty laid-back and calm man. There have only been a couple of times when I actually heard him use the F-word and this was one of those occasions because he was pretty wound up about being lost.

We finally pulled up to the arena and my dad threw open the back door and carried me over his shoulder like a bag of potatoes.

Once we got inside the rink, we could see that our team was already playing—and some poor kid in regular equipment was standing in the crease as our goalie. Without any hesitation, my dad threw me over the glass onto the ice (keep in mind the glass was a lot shorter in the old, local arenas where we played). He didn't wait for a stoppage in play and he didn't care that we would probably get a too-many-men on the ice penalty. My father understood the urgency of the situation and acted accordingly. Amazingly, I landed on my feet when he tossed me over the glass and I simply skated to our net and took my position.

It's memories like those that make me realize how much I loved the game growing up. All those dreaded early-morning practices have left me with a lifetime of memories. In fact, the only other time I can recall my dad using the F-word involved a 6 a.m. hockey practice. My dad used to set the alarm clock for 5 a.m. and wake me up to head out to the rink when we had practices at that time in the morning. We would pack up all my gear the night before so that the morning routine would only involve brushing teeth.

The parents on the team set up a car-pool system so that everyone would rotate driving, because the practices were so early in the morning. But all the parents on the team dreaded picking up Bob Christensen, because he was the only kid on the team who would never be ready. I'm still close friends with Bobo to this day, but he used to drive all the parents nuts because he was so disorganized. When you would pull into his driveway and honk the car horn, that was basically his signal to wake up; the kid never set his alarm clock.

One morning we pulled into Bobo's driveway at 5:15 a.m. and, as usual, all the lights in the house were off and there were no signs of life inside. After honking the car horn, my dad suddenly turned to me and said, "When the fuck is this guy ever going to be on time?" Sure enough, Bobo stumbled out of his house about 10 minutes later and we headed to practice.

Of course, everyone always wants to know, "When did you first realize you wanted to be an NHL goalie?"

For me, it probably happened around the time I was playing bantam hockey. We were starting to take road trips to play tournaments and I fell in love with the idea of doing this for a living.

My most vivid memory from bantam hockey came when we played a tournament against the Notre Dame Hounds. They were the most legendary hockey program in the country at the time and their alumni list is flat-out impressive. Over the years, this tiny prep school in Saskatchewan has produced NHL stars such as Wendel Clark, Rod Brind'Amour and Brad Richards. You didn't choose to go to Notre Dame—they chose you.

So when we had to play them in this bantam tournament, I was fired up. And by "fired up," I mean ridiculously nervous.

I couldn't sleep the whole night before the big game, I was too worried about how I was going to play against the best team in the country. I paced up and down the hallways of the hotel at 4 a.m., which probably wasn't the safest thing for a 13-year-old boy to be doing by himself, in retrospect. But I knew this was a big moment for me in my young career. If I wanted to pursue a career as a professional goalie, then I was going to find out if I had a shred of hope in the next 12 hours.

The experts always tell you that eight hours' sleep is ideal if you want maximum performance as an athlete. But I went into this big game against Notre Dame without a single minute of sleep.

We ended up pulling out a 4–4 tie against them, which was a huge accomplishment for our team. I made more than 40 saves and the performance validated my dream of becoming an

NHL goalie. If I could hold the mighty Notre Dame Hounds to a tie—while working on no sleep—there was hope for me yet.

I'd love to tell you that it was smooth sailing from there and my career took off after the game against Notre Dame. But the life of a young goaltender is filled with highs and lows and during that same season, I suffered the worst humiliation possible for someone in my position: I scored on myself.

We were playing a tournament in Red Deer against their Triple-A bantam team. I was having a pretty bad game where I was really fighting the puck. After I made a routine save, I went to scoop up the rebound and instead of securing it in my glove, I put the puck directly into the net behind me. It was the lowest moment you could experience as a goaltender.

At that point, the coach decided to give me the hook from the game, with very good reason. But since I was just 13 years old, I didn't handle it very well. I came off the ice and I threw my stick. In the process, I swore at our head coach. It wasn't quite a Patrick Roy–Mario Tremblay situation, but it was pretty darn close.

To make matters worse, our coach was a man named Larry Ketsa, who just happened to be the father of my best friend. He was so upset with my actions that he yelled, "Don't you ever swear at me!"

In hindsight, I wasn't even mad at the coach. The swearing and stick-tossing were a reflection of how frustrated I was with my own play. I stood in the hallway tunnel by myself and I started to cry. I had never been pulled from a game before and it really stung. It seems funny to think about scoring on myself now, but at the time there wasn't a worse feeling in the world.

I was fortunate to have a family that really supported me when I had tough times like that. After that particular game in Red Deer, I distinctly remember my dad picking me up to take me home. And this was no ordinary car trip from Red Deer to St. Albert. My dad flew planes as a hobby, so we actually flew home in a little Cessna aircraft after that debacle.

My dad had seen what happened on the ice that day and he told me not to worry. My parents were very good at keeping me even-keeled, which is probably the most important mental quality for a goalie. As we flew back to St. Albert, he told me never to get too high after a win and never to get too low after a loss. I know some kids dread having the car ride home with their father after a bad hockey game. But for me, not only did I have a supportive father, I was the only kid flying home with mine after the game.

Moving on: Junior Hockey and Strange Tales from the Billet House

A couple of years after that bantam tournament, I made a conscious decision to pursue a professional hockey career. The next logical step was to play junior hockey in the Western

Hockey League. I had attracted enough attention to be listed and signed by the Spokane Chiefs. That meant I would have to say goodbye to Edmonton and move to Washington State at the age of 17.

Of course, billets are a very significant part of the junior hockey experience in North America. When you move to a new city as a teenager, into someone else's home, it can be a very intimidating situation. You no longer have Mom's cooking or Dad's advice to look forward to on a daily basis. Everything is brand new—including the family you're living with. It's almost a surreal experience, as your parents and siblings are switched out for a whole new family.

When I went off to Spokane, I was assigned to live with the Emmeritts—a legendary family who always took on billets for the Chiefs. Maryanne and Gene were the mother and father and they also had two grown children—a son named Larry (who lived with us in the house) and a daughter named Wanda (who was older and married). They were all massive Chiefs fans who came to every single home game.

There were four of us being billeted with them at the time: me, Dennis Saharchuk, Marco Fuster and Mike Barlage. We used to have a lot of fun at Larry's expense. We'd often play pranks on him, like putting a glass of water over a door and then calling him into the room. We'd even terrorize Larry in the middle of the night by calling his name through the vents: "Laaaaaaa-rryy, Laaaaaa-ryy." It was the kind of humor you would expect from four teenaged boys who needed to find a way to pass the time with a brand new family. Larry's parents weren't too upset because our pranks were pretty harmless and we made sure to include him in some of the stuff we did around the house.

I also was involved in a strange incident with the Emmeritts' daughter Wanda, when I hit her with a puck before a game. It was during warm-up when both teams were on the ice and I was practicing the art of shoveling a puck on my backhand. I flipped the puck from behind our net and I ended up putting too much on it, because it sailed clear across the arena. I kept my eye on the puck the whole time and, sure enough, it landed squarely on an unsuspecting Wanda, catching her right on the glasses. She went down in pain and was knocked out.

I didn't know what to do. I just kept circling around our half of the rink for warm-up, not taking my eyes off her as she received medical attention. But I didn't skate across to see how my billet's daughter was doing. When I got home that night, Wanda was there, with a huge ice pack on her forehead and her glasses taped up in the middle. She looked like one of the Hanson Brothers.

I didn't know if she realized that I had been the one to shoot the puck that hit her, so I played dumb when I walked into the room.

"Whoa, Wanda—what happened to you?" I asked, feigning surprise.

"You wouldn't believe it, but a puck hit me during the warm-up," she replied.

"That's terrible," I said, quickly leaving the room. She hadn't accused me of anything, and I didn't have the heart to tell her that I was the one responsible. It was a gutless move, but considering how quirky this family was, I didn't want to risk something weird happening if I admitted I was guilty.

You'll understand why I didn't admit to hitting her with the puck when you hear a little more about this family. The Emmeritts lived in a big old house with six bedrooms. Often, they would take on four or five junior players at a time because they had the room to house them all.

They also kept five refrigerators and two deep freezers in the house—which on the surface doesn't sound that strange because they were housing five hungry teenaged hockey players. But the reason they had stocked up on so much food wasn't because we were living there. They were straight out of the military conspiracy school and they believed you needed to stockpile a year's worth of food and supplies. Because naturally, if the enemy is going to strike, the first place they are targeting is Spokane, Washington.

They also had military-like rules and regulations for those who lived in their house. All billets had to abide by the team's curfew policy, but the Emmeritt family took it to a whole different level. If you walked into the house even one minute past your curfew, they had already placed a call to the Chiefs' general manager to notify him of the violation. They liked to keep us under a very close watch, and at times it was extremely creepy.

It wasn't beyond the realm of possibility, for instance, that they'd be listening to your phone calls. The family had another disturbing and strange rule: they didn't allow us to lock our bedroom doors. When we were at school during the day, Maryanne would go through all our stuff, even opening up our mail and reading it before we got home. I started doing little tests where I left a letter in a certain spot in my room and when I came back from school, sure enough, it had been moved.

I didn't mind the fact that they had some rules and regulations, but I felt like this was really crossing the line, so I finally confronted Gene one day and told him that I did not like having my mail and personal belongings inspected.

"I don't want you guys looking through my stuff anymore. I want a lock for my room," I said.

Gene absolutely flipped out on me, saying, "This is our house and you will live by our rules."

"You need to respect my privacy," I argued. "You guys aren't my parents. And I can certainly phone the Chiefs and find another place to live."

A few tense weeks later, I was fortunately traded from Spokane to Lethbridge, so I got out of that strange house. I ended up being billeted with the Dyck family when I got to Lethbridge and it was like night and day from my Spokane experience.

I had played a season of minor hockey in Lethbridge in Triple-A bantam, and my best friend at the time was Joel Dyck. When I got traded to Lethbridge, his family naturally became my billets as Joel was playing for Swift Current and his brother, Mike, was playing for Regina. I was back in familiar territory. For me, when I went to their house it was like I was going home—it just felt comfortable.

I'm in regular contact with the Dyck family to this day and their two sons are still two of my best buds. It was truly bizarre to go from one extreme to the other, but it really gave me an appreciation of what a good billet family can do for your career. I'll always be grateful to the Dyck family for helping me through those formative years.

I don't want to even think about how things might have turned out if I'd spent another year in that house in Spokane.

Junior Teammates: Connections for Life

I was sitting on a WestJet airplane recently on a routine flight from Calgary to Toronto. As I half-listened to the announcements from the flight deck, one sentence came through to me clearly: "And your captain today will be Peter Berthelson."

That caught my attention because I'd had Peter Berthelson as a captain before. Only it wasn't on a WestJet flight—it was on my junior hockey team in Lethbridge. I had the flight attendant hand him my phone number and sure enough it was the same Peter that I had played with and we were able to reconnect.

That's the beauty of the relationships you create when playing junior hockey. Everybody can go their own separate ways, but there is a bond that lasts for a lifetime.

I still keep in touch with former Spokane teammates like Ray Whitney and Travis Green, who ended up having long and distinguished careers in the National Hockey League. I was also really tight with Wes Walz in juniors and, as luck would have it, we were reunited with the Minnesota Wild when we were both 30 years old. It's amazing how the connections to junior hockey keep reappearing on the ice. If you see two opponents chatting at the blue line during a pre-game skate, there's a very good chance they played junior together and are catching up on old times.

It's a brotherhood that lasts for life and we have this unspoken bond with each other. Most of us were 16 or 17 years old and away from home for the first time, so it was really comforting to have a bunch of other guys in the same boat. We did everything together: going to school, eating meals and—of course—traveling on the bus.

Bus trips in the Western Hockey League are about as glamorous as you might think. Imagine a 12-hour ride from Lethbridge to Kamloops in the dead of night, with a bus full of sweaty teenagers who've just finished playing a game. And I played in the era before portable DVD players, iPods and tablet computers, so it made those trips even more excruciating.

Our gear used to travel with us at the bottom of the bus and that always presented problems for my goaltending equipment. After playing the game, I would load my soaking-wet gear into my bag and throw it under the bus. Then, after a nice 12-hour bus ride in minus-30 degree conditions, my pads and blocker would be frozen solid. I used to have to chisel out my gear before the next game and try to defrost it so I wouldn't have an icy glove hand at the opening whistle. And after that game, I would load my gear onto the bus and the cycle would repeat itself for the rest of the road trip.

The schedule was just brutal for us to deal with, as we often played four games in the span of five days. For example, we'd play a home game in Lethbridge on a Wednesday night and then embark on a bus trip that would take us through Saskatoon on Friday night, Prince Albert on Saturday night and finish it off with an afternoon matinee in Moose Jaw on Sunday.

I also received my nickname of "Noodles" from riding the buses in junior hockey. During those 12-hour bus rides, we used to stop at terrible diners and restaurants for team meals. I never liked eating at those places because it felt like the Salisbury steak would be sitting in my throat when I tried to play the next night. So I took to bringing along a Crock-Pot with me on the bus and cooking a little pasta dinner while we were driving. Eventually, my teammates started calling me "Noodles" for my habit of eating Kraft Dinner and other pasta dishes on the road.

When you ride the bus for such long stretches, team chemistry is always put to the test. I remember one of the first times I rode the bus when I was called up to Spokane from midget hockey. I was sitting at the front of the bus—where all the rookies had to double up and sit—while the veterans got their own space at the back. We were playing Monopoly and apparently we were getting too loud for the guys who were trying to sleep in the back.

Our game came to an abrupt halt when this lunatic tough guy came from the back of the bus, grabbed our board game, kicked open the bus window and threw the whole thing out as we were flying down the highway. The board game, the pieces and the fake cash all disappeared into the darkness of the night. Needless to say, this disruption upset everybody on board—including our bus driver. He was actually a pretty tough customer himself, so he pulled the bus over and challenged that lunatic tough guy to a fight. Fortunately, cooler heads prevailed and the next day the bus window was fixed with a piece of plywood. I remember always being afraid of that lunatic and luckily I was sent back to midget after that trip, so I never had to play with him again. Ironically, I did play against him in the pro ranks a few years later, but I was never in a position of having to fight him. But for every bad experience like that board game story, there were always 50 more positive ones to tell about team bonding in junior hockey.

Team chemistry is so critical to the success of a junior team, for a number of reasons. Not only were we spending an unhealthy amount of time riding buses together, but we also had to be very tight on the ice. Back then, major junior games in the Western Hockey League used to be bloodbaths if one team took a three- or four-goal lead. In today's game, there are lots of rules about fighting, headshots and brawls, so the game is played with a more controlled aggression.

But back then, you had to be prepared for a bench-clearing brawl if the score was 4–0. Everybody had to have each other's back and it really taught you a lot about teamwork. That type of chemistry was built both on and off the ice.

And whereas today's players have "team-building" activities to foster that sort of connection, our old-school teams had hazing rituals.

Now, fortunately for me, starting goaltenders often avoided having to go through the routine. Nobody wanted to mess with the psyche of the netminders, so they generally left us out of that sort of thing. But I did witness my fair share of bizarre junior hockey hazing rituals when I played in Spokane and Lethbridge.

We had one event called the Marshmallow Race—which has pretty much turned me off the idea of ever eating a campfire s'more in my lifetime.

Two guys would be sitting on chairs—stark naked, of course. Directly across from them would be two chairs with a marshmallow on each. The object of the game was rather simple: The two naked players had to run across to the other chair to pick up the marshmallow and then race back to their original chair. The whole key to the game was the fact that their hands were tied up with a rope—which meant they had to pick up the marshmallow with their butt cheeks. And the consequence for the loser was predictably catastrophic: They had to eat the other player's marshmallow, which that guy had carried in his butt for a good 30 feet.

When I look back at that whole situation now, it's one of the most disgusting things I can imagine—not to mention how grossly unhealthy it could have been. But that was sort of a different era, where we didn't really care too much about being politically correct and hurting a teammate's feelings. We basically wanted everyone to be part of the team—it's just that sometimes you would have to eat a little ass-marshmallow to fully join the club.

Draft Day and Battling a Mascot in the Minors

After my final junior season with the Lethbridge Hurricanes, I was all set for the NHL Entry Draft in 1991.

Several members of my family accompanied me to the draft in Buffalo and my agent, Art Breeze, brought some of his clients along as well. It was pretty exciting because one of those clients was my friend and teammate from Lethbridge, defenseman Jamie Pushor.

I had been told there were a few teams that were contemplating taking me in the draft. I was ranked as the second-best goaltender available and I had been given indications that the Detroit Red Wings were very interested in me. I had been interviewed by the Red Wings four different times in the months leading up to the draft. Those interviews were conducted by their front office brass and usually had a lot of different question-and-answer type sessions as the team tried to gauge my personality.

So when the Red Wings executives came to the podium to make their second-round pick, I was pretty nervous. I had waited a long time to hear my name called out at the NHL Entry Draft, so this was an amazing moment to be able to share with my family.

"The Detroit Red Wings proudly select, from the Lethbridge Hurricanes of the Western Hockey League, Jamie . . ."

My heart was racing so fast. I was ready to stand up and enjoy my big moment when I stopped cold in my tracks.

"Jamie Pushor" was the name that came over the loudspeaker. Not mine. I played in Lethbridge. My name was Jamie. But this wasn't my big moment.

Fortunately, I didn't stand up prematurely because I would have looked like a complete moron. I stood up to shake Pushor's hand and sat back down.

In the next round, my full name was finally called by the
New York Islanders, a team that had also interviewed me on a
number of occasions. They were a pretty legendary organization and I had a chance to meet with Bill Torrey and Al Arbour
right away. The Islanders told me they had plans for me, but
obviously I would need to get some experience in their farm
system before I could realistically think about making the NHL.

I had a good first training camp and was fifth on the orga-
nizational depth chart for goaltenders. The NHL club would
actually need to carry three netminders that season because
one of them—Mark Fitzpatrick—was battling a rare illness.
I started with the Capital District Islanders in the American
Hockey League, but when Fitzy would get sick and need a con-
ditioning stint, he would come down and that would bump
me to the East Coast Hockey League.

I officially broke into the professional ranks with the
Richmond Renegades of the ECHL in the 1991–92 season, but
I was up and down in different leagues for the whole season.

Minor league professional sports teams are often portrayed
in movies because the stories and characters are so entertaining. Long bus rides, strange characters, quirky buildings and
bizarre fans are all part of the mosaic that make up the weird
and wonderful world of minor league sports in North America.

And having played a few seasons in the American Hockey
League, I can tell you that movies like *Slap Shot* and *Bull Durham*
are pretty accurate. After my final season of junior hockey in

Lethbridge—on my first time called up—I joined the Capital District team on a road trip out in Newfoundland, where we were getting set to play two games against the St. John's Maple Leafs. Because St. John's is so far away from many of the other cities in the AHL, we would often stay and play two consecutive games in their rink. On this particular trip, we were going to play in St. John's on a Tuesday night and then stay over and play a rematch against them two days later.

On this trip, I was really looking forward to impressing the organization's goaltending coach, Billy Smith—who just happened to be the best goalie in Islanders franchise history. In addition to backstopping New York to four consecutive Stanley Cups, Smitty had the reputation of being the nastiest goalie of his generation. They nicknamed him "Battlin' Billy" because of his tendency to take down opposing players who got into his crease. Smitty was such a fierce competitor that he actually refused to shake hands with opposing teams at the end of any playoff series.

When I got word that I was starting the first game in St. John's on the Tuesday night, Smith came over to have a nice chat with me. He didn't have any special motivational speech for me, he simply told me to go out there, be aggressive and stop the puck.

The first period went about as well as I could have scripted in my first game with a new team. I made a bunch of saves and we scored a couple of goals, giving us a lead after 20 minutes.

After the intermission wrapped up, I headed back onto the ice with my teammates for the second period. This time, we had to do the long skate across the ice, since we would be occupying the St. John's end of the ice for the middle frame. As I completed the 200-foot skate and neared the goal, I realized that somebody was occupying my crease.

It wasn't an arena worker, making sure the ice conditions were right. And it wasn't the referee making sure the goalposts were snapped in correctly. Instead, standing in my blue paint was none other than "Buddy"—the oversized and feathered mascot of the St. John's Maple Leafs. I've dealt with a lot of things in my crease over the years, but seeing a six-foot bird with a giant head was certainly a first. Buddy was technically a puffin—the provincial bird of Newfoundland. He looked like a cross between a penguin and Toucan Sam, the spokesman for Froot Loops cereal.

As I pulled up to take my spot, I realized that Buddy was trying to taunt me. He was shaking his feathered arms, as if to put a hex on me. The crowd was roaring with delight, loving the fact that their hometown mascot was trying to get under the skin of the opposing goaltender.

I tried not to make too big a deal of it, so I simply took my spot in the net, giving Buddy a slight nudge to get out of the way. And wouldn't you know it—the damn mascot pushed me back.

I was starting to wonder, "What is wrong with this guy?" Only in the AHL can you have a professional goalie engaged in a physical confrontation with a mascot, just moments before the puck is about to be dropped. Finally, Buddy took the hint and left the area, finding his spot in the crowd to entertain the fans.

As the second period started, I was able to get focused quickly and concentrate on the game. I actually ended up being really sharp the rest of the night, during a 5–2 win for our squad. I think I made in the neighborhood of 35 saves and was named the game's first star in the building.

Walking into the dressing room, I couldn't wait to get some feedback from Billy Smith. I was sure that he would be impressed with the technical aspect of my game. And, sure enough, Smitty was waiting for me at my stall.

"I need to talk to you," he said, pulling me quickly into the hallway.

I was a little bit confused as to why he had to praise me in private. I had just been named the first star of the game— surely he could talk about my effort in front of my teammates.

Then Billy Smith started to read me the riot act.

"Don't you ever let a mascot stand in your crease. That is your space and you control it," he said.

"But, Billy, I had a great game," I protested.

"I don't care how many pucks you stop. Don't you ever let a fucking mascot stand in your crease," he countered. Smitty was getting so angry, I was wondering if he was going to seek out this oversized puffin himself.

And then Billy Smith issued me a direct challenge.

"If he's there next game, you fucking run him over. Do you understand?"

I think I mumbled some sort of response, which indicated to Billy that I would follow through on his order. But on the inside, I was terrified. I was 20 years old and had just been ripped to shreds by an NHL legend. And this was after I was named the first star of the game. I was so impressionable and vulnerable at the time, I remember thinking that I just wanted to go and hide out somewhere.

I had a pretty restless night of sleep after the game, wondering if I would actually follow through on my promise to abuse Buddy the mascot on Thursday night.

But as I woke up on Wednesday morning, I had another thought pop into my mind: What if I didn't play on Thursday night? That would be the perfect scenario for me. Coaches often like to split playing time for the goalies in the AHL and I was thinking there was a very good chance I could watch Thursday's game from the end of the bench.

So all during Wednesday's practice, I tried to avoid making eye contact with our head coach, Butch Goring. I figured that if Butch didn't see me, he wouldn't tab me as the starter. Out of sight, out of mind, right?

We had pretty much wrapped up the one-hour session when Butch skated over to me and tapped my pads. "You're starting tomorrow night, kid."

Those are five words that most young goalies love to hear. But this was one time when I was actually wishing to be a spectator.

The next 24 hours were pretty much a blur. I usually have a set routine for getting ready for a game, but I have no recollection of my preparation for the rematch with St. John's. I wasn't thinking about my game, the opponent or anything of that nature. I was just worried about that damn mascot.

I tried to convince myself that maybe Buddy wouldn't be at the arena this time. But it seemed like flawed logic to assume that Buddy the mascot only worked on Tuesdays. I really didn't know what I'd do if Buddy was standing in my crease again to start the second period. I was so rattled by the whole situation that I allowed three goals in the first period. I was shaky, but now the moment of truth had arrived.

As the gates opened up for the second period, I looked across the ice and, sure enough, Buddy the mascot was waiting for me in my crease. I wasn't sure what I was going to do. Smitty had told me to knock him out of there, but this was a cartoon bird we were talking about.

Then I noticed that Buddy was doing that hex thing again, taunting me with his arms.

And then I made the decision: I am going to bury this bird.

I started skating at full speed from 150 feet away, gaining speed like I never had before. And I made a direct line for Buddy, who probably thought I didn't have the stones to pull this off.

As I got closer to the crease, Buddy had yet to vacate the blue paint. I could hear the words of Smitty echoing in my head as I got closer: "If he's there next game, you fucking run him over."

And so, without breaking stride once, I absolutely bowled over Buddy the mascot—sending him spinning into the corner. I'm pretty sure I knocked his head off the costume, but I was so charged up I didn't even look over.

Now the crowd started to get on me, booing and taunting me. I'm sure they didn't know about the previous history between me and the puffin, but that probably would have mattered little to them anyway. Buddy—who thankfully did not sustain any major injuries—slinked off the ice and the game started again.

My shaky play from the first period continued for the rest of the night. I think I allowed six or seven goals in a blowout loss. Whereas I was the first star of the game on Tuesday night, I was probably the worst player on the ice in the second game.

After the game, I was now expecting to get another tongue-lashing from Billy Smith. My angles were off, my rebound control was shaky and I was just terrible from most technical aspects.

Once again, Smitty was waiting for me at my stall as I walked into the visitors' locker room. This time, he was grinning from ear to ear.

"That's how you do it, kid. That's how you become a man in this league. That's how you get respect," he said, only concerned about my handling of the mascot.

And I'm sure in his report back to the Islanders that night, Smitty would have only positive things to say about my compete level—despite the fact I gave up six goals.

Both as a goalie and as a coach, Battlin' Billy cared more about the blue paint than anybody else I've ever met. He taught me the importance of working on my mental game as much as my technical game. I never forgot his advice and he certainly helped me become a better goalie as my career advanced into the NHL.

First Taste of NHL Action

In the fall of 1991, I attended my first-ever professional training camp. Right away, I figured I would never play a single game in the National Hockey League. These guys were so big and strong, I had never seen anything like them before. Steve Thomas and Pat Flatley were shooting the puck at me at terrifying speeds.

I managed to settle my nerves and by the end of training camp, I actually won the award for the top rookie. It was exciting and an honor to win this award—the $75 bonus didn't hurt either.

The Islanders assigned me to the minors, but I had a positive feeling about where my career was headed. I knew I had a lot of work to do to reach the NHL, but I was really excited to be a professional hockey player.

I had no expectations that I would be back playing in Long Island any time that season. But all of that changed with a phone call that woke me up at 2 a.m. one day in late March. It was the Islanders calling to let me know that they needed my services immediately. I had been shuttling between the Richmond club and the Capital District squad that season and at this point, I was currently with the East Coast League affiliate.

Up in New York, Glenn Healy had been hurt the night before, and for some reason they could not get hold of their top AHL goaltender Danny Lorenz. So they turned to me as their next-best option, and suddenly I had a chance to suit up for an NHL game. They needed me to get on an 8 a.m. flight to New York and serve as the backup that night against the Red Wings.

I was in total scramble mode, not quite believing that I would be dressing for my first NHL game later that same day. I got to the airport in Richmond, waiting for my flight to New York. As I was sitting in the departures lounge, I could see our plane coming in for a landing. All of a sudden, this plane hits a flock of birds and has a mechanical failure when it lands. There were feathers everywhere. Nobody got hurt, but this was supposed to be the plane that was taking me to New York. Naturally, the flight got canceled. Just my luck—I'm supposed to make my NHL debut and my outbound plane hits a flock of birds.

The airline was able to reroute me through Washington, D.C., but the problem was my new flight was scheduled to land at LaGuardia Airport in New York at 6:30 p.m. That would give me just one hour to get from the airport to the rink for the start of the game.

Fortunately, I was good friends with an off-duty cop from New Jersey named Rick Adams, who happened to be in New York at the time. He picked me up at the airport and drove at about 100 mph to get me to the Nassau Coliseum. I got inside the rink and was running through the hallways with my equipment, trying to make it on time. By the time I got to the dressing room area, the players were coming off the ice from warm-ups.

I was forced to do some very quick introductions to some teammates I hadn't met before.

"Hi, I'm Jamie," I remember saying to Ray Ferraro inside the dressing room.

Ray, who has always been very quick-witted, responded by saying, "Did you not get the memo that this game starts at 7:30?"

I was stunned, with nothing to say in reply, since I was a starstruck rookie. But then I realized that Ray was joking with me. He smiled and said, "Settle in, kid, and get dressed. But be ready to play, because this goalie has been awful lately," he said, teasing Steve Weeks, who was starting that night.

I sat on the end of the bench that evening and, fortunately, I was not pressed into action.

The next day, with Healy still hurt, I flew with the team for my first-ever road trip to Toronto. This time, I didn't have problems with the airplane, but I did experience a different type of turbulence.

When we landed in Toronto, it turned out to be the day on which the NHL Players' Association called for a strike vote. There had been a lot of talk that the union was going to strike before the playoffs and now the situation with the league owners had come to a head.

So here I am with exactly 24 hours of NHL experience under my belt and I'm voting on whether or not the union should go on strike. The players actually voted overwhelmingly in favor of a strike by a margin of 560 to 4. However, the work stoppage did not last long—only 10 days in total—before the regular season and playoffs resumed without incident.

Once the strike ended, Glenn Healy was healthy again and I was back down in the minors. But my first call-up to the National Hockey League was certainly a memorable experience. How many other players in NHL history can say their first call-up involved birds hitting an airplane and a work stoppage?

2

Hextall, the Chicken and Other Tales from My Goalie Partners like Luongo and Kiprusoff

After a couple of years of improving my game in the minors, I was ready to make the jump to the NHL for the 1993–94 season. When I finally reached the NHL for the first time as a regular goaltender, I was glad to be part of the New York Islanders organization. The Islanders had made a surprising run to the conference finals the previous year before finally being eliminated by the Montreal Canadiens.

But as we opened training camp in the fall of 1993, the club had a brand-new look in goal. Glenn Healy and Mark Fitzpatrick, who had split the goaltending duties during the 1992–93 season, had both moved on to new teams. Fitzpatrick had been traded to the Quebec Nordiques at the NHL Entry Draft in June in exchange for Ron Hextall.

Of course, when I first heard that I was competing for ice time with Ron Hextall, I was a little bit nervous. After all, while Hextall was known for being the best puck-handling goalie in hockey history, he was equally famous for being the most temperamental netminder to ever step inside the crease.

I was looking forward to learning some of the tricks of the trade from Hextall—especially those puck-handling skills. Hexy completely revolutionized the game, as he was essentially a third defenseman on the ice. He changed the way that teams could forecheck because suddenly the goalie had become an active puck-handler.

I remember going out onto the ice with him and he could shoot the puck just as well as a forward. He would choke down on his goalie stick and take slap shots that would ring off the crossbar as if they were shot from a composite stick. Even though he was the pioneer, Hextall is still the best puck-handling goaltender the NHL has ever seen.

However, stability and Hexy weren't exactly phrases that were often used in the same sentence when he was playing, so I certainly played the part of the intimidated 22-year-old rookie when Hexy showed up to the Islanders training camp. His memorable, two-handed lumberjack slash on Kent Nilsson during the Stanley Cup final in 1987 showed just how vicious he could be on the ice. Many fans also remember watching Hextall lose his cool and attack Chris Chelios at the end of a playoff series a couple of years after that.

Hexy was such a competitor that he didn't even like it when teammates would score on him during practice. I remember Ray Ferraro once scoring against him during a breakaway drill and Hexy was so upset that he took the puck and shot it at Ferraro's head when he skated back to the corner. The upside of his fierce nature was that he had a competitive fire that was infectious inside the dressing room.

But to my complete surprise, Hexy was a totally different person once he stepped off the ice. The lunatic version of Ron Hextall—the one that most people were familiar with—only seemed to come out when he strapped on his pads. Away from the rink, Ron was one of the best role models a young goalie could ask for. He was willing to share his secrets of the trade, even though I was a rookie who was trying to take playing time away from him. He taught me some invaluable things about work ethic and how to be a pro, lessons that would stay with me for the rest of my career. And for those reasons, Ron Hextall will always be one of my favorite people in the game of hockey.

However, I did get a chance to see the side of Ron Hextall that everybody is familiar with during a road trip to St. Louis in early March of my rookie year.

After finishing up our morning skate, we boarded a bus and headed back to the hotel for our team lunch. Nowadays,

NHL team meals are giant buffet spreads, filled with steaks, chicken breasts, salmon and a variety of pastas and salads to choose from. But back in the early 1990s, NHL teams used to sit down for meals and be served by waiters and waitresses, just like you would in a restaurant.

So on this particular day, I grabbed a seat at a table with Ray Ferraro, Pat Flatley, Steve Thomas and Hexy. Ron treated me very well and I used to love to sit with him at pre-game meals and take in the conversation, as well as watch his preparation, even though it was technically a veteran table.

On game days, however, it was a pretty well-known fact that you didn't speak to Ron unless he spoke to you first. Like most goalies, he would get into a bit of a zone in the hours leading up to puck-drop.

All of us sitting at the table were wearing our suits, since dress codes are usually strictly enforced by NHL teams on the road. But Ron took exceptional pride in the suit he was wearing on this day, bragging to us that he had paid well over a thousand dollars for the outfit. (Remember that 20 years ago it was a big deal to pay a thousand dollars for a suit.) But thanks to our waiter, Ron picked the worst possible day to wear his most expensive suit.

The young man serving us lunch was completely out of his element in a room full of 20 NHL hockey players. As he was leaning over to deliver Pat Flatley his lunch, he ended up accidentally dropping two half-chickens right onto Hexy's lap.

And these were rotisserie chickens that were full of oil and juices, so the whole thing made quite a mess on Ron's new suit.

To make matters worse, the waiter tried to clean up the mess by grabbing a nearby set of napkins and trying to rub Hexy down to remove the stains. And of course this poor waiter had no idea that he was dealing with one of the most temperamental and combative goalies to ever play in the National Hockey League.

"Get the fuck away from me," Hexy barked at him.

The entire room fell silent at this point, as all of my teammates were eager to see how the interaction between Ron Hextall and the waiter was going to play out.

The waiter felt awful at this point, apologizing profusely every few seconds. He even offered to pay for the dry cleaning to the damaged suit.

"Just get away from me. I'll be fine," Hexy repeated, this time giving the waiter the death stare that he usually reserved for opposing forwards who got near his crease. Finally, the waiter—who was visibly upset and shaken—complied with Hexy's wishes and retreated to the kitchen.

At that point, Hexy turned to me and said, "You better be ready to go tonight, kid, because I'm going to fucking kill somebody."

I remember thinking that perhaps Hexy's warning to me was just a heat of the moment thing. After all, he'd just had his favorite suit ruined by a clumsy waiter and a $20 plate of chicken. By the time the game rolled around that night, Hexy would have regained his cool and everything would be just fine, right?

But there was also a part of me that figured I had better be ready to step into action because this was Ron Hextall we were talking about. And if he mentioned the fact that he was going to kill someone that night, there was probably a pretty good chance he was going to follow through on that threat.

As we stepped onto the ice that night against the Blues, I was prepared for anything. Inside the old rink in St. Louis, the backup goaltender actually sat behind the home net in the Zamboni entrance; there wasn't enough room for an extra body at the end of the visitors' bench.

The Blues were one of the most highly skilled and offensive teams in the NHL at the time, with the likes of Brett Hull, Brendan Shanahan and Craig Janney. And just a few days before this game, they had completed a trade with the Vancouver Canucks to acquire Petr Nedved, adding yet another potent offensive weapon.

Sure enough, just after the opening drop of the puck, the Blues offensive went to work.

They scored once. They scored twice. And before the game was even 10 minutes old, Petr Nedved made it 3–0 for the home team. And this apparently was Hexy's breaking point, because as soon as that third goal went in, he started chasing

Nedved around the rink—attempting to fulfill his earlier promise of killing somebody.

I was watching from my seat in near disbelief when I realized that our head coach, Al Arbour, was waving at me and motioning for me to get into the net. The end boards swung open and I quickly put on my mask and headed onto the ice.

I had to skate right past the Blues home net, which was directly in front of me. As I did, Curtis Joseph said to me, "Good luck, kid. Have some fun." I always marveled at how relaxed and comfortable CuJo was on the ice.

That laid-back demeanor was in direct contrast to Hexy, who had been immediately ejected from the game for chasing Nedved around with his stick. And the referees had no idea that this was pretty much a premeditated attack from Hexy, dating back to the lunchtime incident.

I crossed paths with Hexy around centre ice and he didn't even make eye contact with me. He was in a completely different zone. His statistical line for the day: 3 goals, 10 shots, 9:12 of playing time and one damaged designer suit.

Suddenly, I'm thrown into the middle of an NHL game and I realize that it's going to be me in goal for the next 50 minutes—because we don't have any other options. Hexy's already hit the showers and I have the pleasure of trying to silence one of the best offensive teams in the league. I'm only a few months into my NHL career at this point, so I'm still in awe of guys like Hull and Shanahan on the ice.

And just my luck, the first shot I face is a blistering one-timer from Brett Hull in the slot. No word of a lie, the puck hit my shoulder and bounced into the corner before I even had time to react. It felt nice to stop the best sniper in the NHL and so my confidence grew as the game progressed. We erased the three-goal deficit thanks to a couple of goals from Stevie Thomas, and we finished the game in a 5–5 tie.

After the game, I was feeling pretty good about myself. When I saw Hexy in the locker room, I was thinking he might actually congratulate me on such a fine relief performance. Instead, there were no kind words coming my way—only a unique apology. He came up to me and said, with a hint of a grin—almost a smirk, "Sorry about that, kid. It was the fucking chicken's fault." And then he just walked away.

It was classic Ron Hextall. One of the best people around—provided you didn't cross him. Or drop a chicken in his lap.

Playing with Grant Fuhr— A Dream Come True

When I was 12 years old, I participated in a contest called the Dairy Queen Shootout. During the intermission of Edmonton Oilers home games, they would have a breakaway contest involving local kids. At the end of the season, the winner of the Dairy Queen Shootout would get to have his picture taken with a member of the Oilers.

As luck would have it, I ended up winning the contest that season and the team invited me down for its first home playoff game. Since Andy Moog was the starting goalie that night, I got my picture taken with Grant Fuhr on the ice during the first intermission. As a doughy and roly-poly kid, I was completely in awe of being next to a professional goalie as talented as Fuhr. In the next few years, I followed closely as he became the backbone of the Oilers's Stanley Cup teams and I cherished that photograph even more.

Now fast forward about 15 years from the night of that photo and suddenly I'm Grant Fuhr's goalie partner with the St. Louis Blues. It was a totally surreal experience for me to have the chance to play alongside one of my boyhood idols.

And Grant even got a kick out of the story about us having that Dairy Queen Shootout connection. The first time we went back to Edmonton with the Blues, I went for breakfast in the lobby of the Hotel Macdonald. Grant was sitting at a table and he flagged me down.

"Hey, chum, looks like we're getting a little bit of press today," he said with a big smile on his face.

Grant was holding up a copy of that morning's *Edmonton Sun*. On the front page of the sports section was the photo of me and Grant from the Dairy Queen Shootout 15 years earlier. The newspaper had tracked down a copy of the picture and the editor thought it was neat that a kid from St. Albert had a chance to be teammates with a goaltending legend.

Once the initial awe of playing with Fuhr wore off, I quickly realized he was a completely down-to-earth guy. There was never any of the arrogance and attitude you might expect from a goaltender who had won multiple Stanley Cups.

I was always struck by how calm and relaxed he was before every single game, no matter what was at stake. Whenever I was Fuhr's backup, I would spend a lot of time in the trainer's room before the game, eating popcorn and just shooting the breeze with the guys. And even though he was the starting goalie, Fuhr would routinely come in and start eating my popcorn— just a few minutes before puck-drop. He was like a big kid all the time.

When we played together in St. Louis, my job was to make sure that Grant got a breather every few games. As a backup goalie, it's your duty to make sure you give the starter a complete night off on those occasions. The last thing you want to do is have an off night and force the starter to come in on his scheduled night off.

One time in Montreal, we were playing the Habs and I was given the start by coach Joel Quenneville. Since Grant knew he wasn't playing that night, he started eating those famous Montreal hot dogs as soon as we got to the rink.

He kept pestering me as we were out for the pre-game skate at 7 p.m. "Chum, how are you doing—are you going to be okay tonight?" he asked. All he wanted to do was eat hot dogs. So once I told him I was totally fine, it basically gave him the green light to eat as many hot dogs as he wanted. I think he wolfed down four or five hot dogs right after the warm-up.

But another time in Philadelphia, I did make Fuhr come in and play on one of his scheduled nights off. I was really sick, but I didn't say anything to the coaching staff. It was early in the season and I wanted to make sure I got some playing time.

I was doing fine as the game started, but my flu symptoms got progressively worse. By the midway point of the second period, I hadn't allowed a single goal—but I could barely stand up. I made a save and then my body started to experience severe cramping. I couldn't even get back to my feet and so the training staff had to rush onto the ice to help me out.

I remember looking up and seeing Fuhr out on the ice with a big jawbreaker in his mouth. "Hey, chum, are you okay? Do you need me to come in?" he asked.

While I tried to formulate an answer, I just kept staring at him and his jawbreaker. It was one of the funniest things I had ever seen; a Hall of Fame goaltender so relaxed that he's eating candy before potentially being thrown into an NHL game.

This was one of those situations where I couldn't keep playing, so it forced him to finish off his jawbreaker and take over in goal. And naturally, we ended up beating the Flyers 3–2 that night with Fuhr getting credit for the win.

His laid-back approach was sometimes a direct contrast to the attitude held by some of the other players on our team—most notably Chris Pronger. It was amazing for me to see how two Hall of Fame players, who were the best at their respective positions, could have such different approaches to the game. If Fuhr represented the cool and calm style of the game, then Pronger was definitely the epitome of fire and intensity.

At the tail end of the 1997–98 season, Pronger was battling for the plus/minus lead in the NHL with Nicklas Lidstrom and Larry Murphy of the Detroit Red Wings. This award meant a lot to Pronger, for a couple of different reasons. Not only would there be the prestige of leading the NHL in plus/minus, but there was also a significant contract bonus that kicked in if he won the award. If I recall, it was in the neighborhood of $1 million, so Pronger had a vested interest in finishing first in the NHL in this category.

We're playing against the Sharks one night in a fairly meaningless game in the standings, but this game carries some importance for Pronger in his pursuit of the plus/minus lead. We're up 5–1 in the third period and Stephane Matteau scores a totally ugly goal for San Jose against Fuhr from the corner. This goal had no business going in; it was a total fluke that it beat Fuhr. Of course, Pronger happened to be on the ice and because it was an even-strength goal from Matteau, it hurt Pronger's plus/minus. Pronger was livid at Fuhr and he broke his stick on the ice in frustration.

He then yelled over at me on the bench, "Tell that fucker to wake the fuck up!" Of course, I wasn't going to relay that message to my goaltending partner. And when I looked over at Fuhr, I could see him smiling behind his mask. We were winning the game 5–2 and that's all he was really concerned about.

A couple of minutes later, there was a TV timeout and Fuhr skated over to our bench. Pronger was still fuming about the earlier Sharks goal.

"Wake the fuck up!" Pronger told Fuhr, this time delivering the message himself.

Fuhr, however, still found the whole situation amusing. "You mouth off at me one more time and I might have to let another one go in," he said with a smile. He put his mask back on and returned to his crease to finish the game. It was an amazing interaction between two Hall of Fame players who had risen to the top of their game, each in his own unique way.

And for the record, Pronger did end up winning the plus/minus award that season with a +47 rating. So the whole Matteau goal fiasco just turned out to be a funny footnote that did not cost him anything.

While Fuhr had a laid-back persona, he did have an internal drive that he rarely showed off in public. But when he did, he could completely captivate a room.

In the first round of the 1999 playoffs, we were trailing the Phoenix Coyotes 3–1 in our series. We were on the verge of elimination and Fuhr hadn't been playing his best up to that point in the series. He was really struggling physically, with his back and knees bothering him. Fuhr was torched for a total of nine goals in Games 2 and 3 of the series and it looked like we were toast against the Coyotes.

With our team facing elimination, we pulled out a 2–1 overtime win in Game 5. Fuhr was brilliant on that night, stopping 26 shots, and his confidence seemed to snowball from there. We won Game 6 on home ice, setting up a do-or-die Game 7 in Phoenix.

Fuhr had been in a lot of Game 7 situations before, including winning the Stanley Cup, so none of us were worried about his mental state heading into this pivotal contest. But as we sat inside the locker room before puck-drop, Fuhr made a comment to the team—something he rarely ever did.

"Boys, just get me one goal tonight and I've got it from there," he boldly declared.

I had never seen anything like it during my professional career. Here was a goaltender basically guaranteeing a shutout in Game 7 of a Stanley Cup playoff series. To me, this was like Babe Ruth calling his home run shot or Mark Messier guaranteeing that the Rangers were going to win in 1994. And because Fuhr rarely stood up and spoke, his message carried even more weight inside the room. Not a single one of us doubted that Grant Fuhr could post a shutout in a Game 7.

After 60 minutes of regulation time, the game was still tied 0–0. Then, late in the first overtime period, Pierre Turgeon tipped in a shot from Scott Young past Nikolai Khabibulin for the winning goal and we eliminated the Coyotes with a 1–0 victory. For 77 minutes and 59 seconds, Grant Fuhr held true to his word. He did not allow a single puck to get past him, making 35 saves until our offense could finally muster a goal. It was one of the most amazing goaltending displays I had ever witnessed—made even more remarkable by the fact that Fuhr had guaranteed it a couple of hours earlier.

I was so fortunate to be able to play a couple of seasons with Grant Fuhr. It allowed me to see how he handled pressure situations in his own unique way. To this day, I still look at him with the same admiration and respect that I did when I was 12 years old.

Running over Roberto Luongo with a Zamboni

I have to thank Roberto Luongo for making me famous on Canadian television. When I was his backup in Florida, TSN's James Duthie came down to do a spoof story on our relationship. Because Roberto played more than 70 games per season, James thought it would be funny to do a piece on how I was secretly jealous of Roberto's playing time.

We set up a whole bunch of staged scenarios—where I was spoon-feeding Roberto his lunch, tying his skates, doing his grocery shopping and pedaling the exercise bike for him. Basically, Roberto was bossing me around and I was following his orders because he was the undisputed number-one goalie and I was his lowly backup. But part of the spoof included a scene where I had a fantasy of running Roberto over with the Zamboni—so that I could be the number-one netminder for the Florida Panthers. (Fortunately for everyone in the organization, we used a dummy instead of Roberto when we shot the scene of me running him over with the Zamboni.)

It was a brilliant piece of television by James and it really helped give me some exposure on television—which probably helped when I had to make some post-career decisions. But that spoof story also showed off a side of Roberto Luongo that fans often don't see: his funny side. Roberto has a wicked sense of humor, a sharp wit that he will use against his teammates and close friends.

He used to hate playing cards with me on the back of the Panthers' charter plane, because I wouldn't take the game as seriously as he did. Roberto is one of the most intense and competitive poker players in the National Hockey League. You'll often see him in those celebrity poker tournaments because he loves to play so much. But I was one of those poker players who had ADD or a short attention span, so I couldn't get engaged in a game for longer than 15 or 20 minutes. And when I'd get bored or frustrated with the game, I would simply lay my cards on the table and go all-in.

This would frustrate Roberto to no end because I would often beat him by going all-in—and he hated the fact that I took all the strategy and decision-making out of the game. He would rip me and curse a blue streak when I beat him, vowing that he would never play cards with me again.

That competitive streak in poker games can often be seen on the ice, where Roberto has established himself as a Hall-of-Fame netminder. He finally started getting proper recognition once he went to Vancouver and helped transform the Canucks franchise into a Stanley Cup contender. But when he was with the Panthers, Roberto was pretty much a man on an island.

He set an NHL record by facing 2,475 shots during the 2003–04 season in Florida. There were nights where we were getting outshot 50 to 20 and yet Roberto gave us a chance to win. The amazing thing about Roberto is that he never complained and pointed fingers at his teammates, despite the fact that the ice was so tilted. One night when I backed him up, I remember we gave up 29 shots in a single period. Roberto only gave up one goal and we were still in the hockey game.

As he came into the dressing room, you could see that he was mentally and physically exhausted. Remember that some goalies like Marty Turco in Dallas or Martin Brodeur in New Jersey were routinely facing 18 or 20 shots through the course of an entire game. And here was Roberto, taking 29 shots in a single period of hockey.

But when he walked into the room, he didn't complain out loud like a lot of goalies would do in that situation. I remember he just took off his gear and said, "Hey, guys, we are a lot better than this."

And that was the end of his speech. He didn't say, "Hey, guys, is anyone else out there playing with me?" or, "Hey, guys, it must be nice to not break a sweat."

Even though he was one of the premier goalies in the league—and had certainly earned the right to blow up at his teammates—he simply chose to make a simple, quiet and understated comment to the room. He didn't point at Stephen Weiss or Jay Bouwmeester and rip them in front of the whole group.

Roberto is a perfectionist, but he tries really hard to keep those expectations on himself. I remember another time when he was going through a particularly tough stretch in Florida and I was trying to help him iron out his issues. He had lost three or four games in a row and I volunteered to assist him with some pre-practice drills.

"Hey, why don't we come to the rink early tomorrow and we'll work on the ice together," I offered.

"No thanks, Noodles," he said. "I think I need to come to the rink and do some stuff by myself."

So the next morning, I came to the rink early—and, sure enough, Roberto was already on the ice. This was a good

90 minutes before the team was supposed to hit the ice for practice. Since he wanted to work by himself, I was very intrigued by what drills he could do without a shooter or goalie partner on the ice.

I snuck underneath the stands and found a little crack through the glass where I could watch him on the ice. Roberto was in full gear, visualizing situations that would happen during the course of the game. He was going post-to-post, he was pretending to stop a wraparound and he was coming out of his crease to challenge imaginary shooters. I had never seen anything like this before; a star goaltender in the NHL was on the ice by himself, going through the ghost exercise of a game.

That morning I went back and forth between the locker room and the practice ice and I watched Roberto do this for almost an hour. You sometimes hear stories about how Kobe Bryant will go and shoot three-pointers for an hour by himself in an empty gym after the Lakers lose a game. This was pretty much the hockey equivalent, as Roberto worked on his technical routine without anyone else watching—except for me.

He's been nominated for the Hart Trophy, Vezina Trophy and Lester B. Pearson Award during the course of his career, all great indicators that he is one of the best goaltenders of all time. But unfortunately for Roberto, there are always lingering doubts about his ability to win the big game or come through in the pressure situation.

I was so happy for him when he backstopped Team Canada to a gold medal at the Winter Olympics in 2010. I had a lot of close friends on that team like Jarome Iginla and Chris Pronger, but I was probably the happiest for Roberto. I don't think you could have a more pressure-packed situation, playing for a gold medal on home ice while an entire country watched your every move. In my mind, Roberto passed that test with flying colors and has the gold medal to prove it.

I really wanted him to also win the Stanley Cup the following year with the Canucks, so I was really disappointed when Vancouver lost Games 6 and 7 of the final to the Boston Bruins. I know Roberto took a lot of heat for the loss—and his controversial comments about Tim Thomas—but you have to understand how much this guy wanted to win for the city.

I've had the good fortune of spending time with Roberto and his family at Thanksgiving and Christmas and I can honestly tell you he is one of the most genuine people in the game of hockey. My sincere wish for him is that he wins that Stanley Cup someday and that the hockey world can finally see him in the same light as I do.

Roberto has been traded twice in his career and both teams that dealt him away—the New York Islanders and Florida Panthers—came to regret the move. And perhaps that is one of the greatest compliments you could pay to Roberto Luongo.

Miikka Kiprusoff Jinxes My Shutout

After my playing career wrapped up, I had a chance to pursue a career as a goaltending coach with the Calgary Flames. In my first season on the job, I was tasked with the easiest job in professional sports: keeping Miikka Kiprusoff happy.

After spending a couple of seasons as his goaltending partner, I knew exactly what made Miikka tick. He's the most easygoing, mild-mannered goaltender that you will ever come across. Whereas a guy like Ron Hextall wore his emotions on his sleeve, Miikka kept his to himself when he was inside the blue paint. I feel very privileged to be one of the few people who knows exactly what Miikka is thinking underneath his mask.

Early in that first season as goalie coach, I was in a meeting with Brent Sutter and the other assistants, Dave Lowry, Ryan McGill and Rob Cookson. We were having a closed-door session as coaches often do, trying to hash out some personnel issues we had on the team. There was a knock at the door and one of our trainers said that Miikka needed to speak with me right away. Since this appeared to be an urgent matter, Brent Sutter excused me from the meeting. "Go and see what's up with him," he instructed me.

So I headed to the back area of the dressing room to find Miikka and see what he needed from me. Since this was a game day, I figured he might want to go over some pre-scouting questions about our opponent. Or maybe he wanted to break down some video with me and go over some technical issues.

I walked into the room and found Miikka in front of the computer with some goaltending video on the screen. But upon closer inspection, he was actually on YouTube.

"Jamie, you have to check out this video. It's hilarious!" he said as I approached the screen.

"Miikka, you just pulled me out of a meeting with the coaches."

"Yeah, but trust me—this is really funny."

So he proceeded to hit the play button. The video showed a European goalie's weird celebration after winning a shoot-out. The goalie makes the save and then pulls his own jersey over his head and skates around with his goalie stick turned upside-down—using it as a cane, as if he's a blind person.

To Miikka, this was the funniest thing in the world and he had to share it with me immediately. We ended up watching the video clip probably 30 times and we were laughing so hard we were forced to shut the door and close the blinds so nobody could see what we were doing. I figured Brent Sutter would not be impressed to find out that we were surfing YouTube clips rather than breaking down goalie video that pertained to our game that night.

Of course Miikka was great in the game that night and I was sure to credit our special little video session for his success. But that is the essence of Miikka Kiprusoff. On the one hand, he's a joking prankster who loves to laugh; on the other, he is a world-class goaltender with unmatched focus and determination.

His work ethic is unparalleled and it's a big reason why he's won more than 300 games as a goaltender. You can find him stretching for almost three hours every day to make sure his body is in peak condition. As a former goaltender myself, I can tell you that stretching for more than 45 minutes at a time is a mental grind as much as a physical one. But Miikka thinks nothing of doing the splits for two hours a day, just to make sure his body is in optimal game shape.

He does like to relax in the off-season and I've had the pleasure of going over to Finland and spending time with him in the summer. He's very quiet and laid-back; he just enjoys fishing and hanging out by the lake with his good friends. Miikka is so quiet and unassuming off the ice that you'd never suspect he's one of the greatest goaltenders of his generation.

My favorite story about Miikka and his ability to be simultaneously laid-back and fiery comes from a regular season game when I was serving as his backup with the Flames.

Our trainer, Mark DePasquale, had recently bought his kids a pet guinea pig for Christmas. For some reason, this guinea pig—named Lightning—had only one eye. Miikka found endless humor in this fact, and he would often tease Mark by saying, "Were you too cheap to buy one with two eyes?"

Other times, Mark would come into the locker room to talk to Miikka about his equipment and halfway through the conversation, Miikka would close one of his eyes. He loved to remind Mark about the guinea pig in every situation you could imagine.

One night we were playing a game that was tied late in the third period. During the final TV timeout, Miikka skated over to the bench and lifted his mask to take a drink of water. Miikka closed one of his eyes as he was having his drink and he made sure that Mark could see him. Here he was in the middle of a pressure-packed game in the National Hockey League and Miikka was making fun of our trainer's one-eyed guinea pig.

So the next time you see him lift up his mask during a game, make sure to notice if he's got one eye closed. If he does, you'll be in on the inside joke about the one-eyed guinea pig.

I've also been on the receiving end of one of Kipper's jokes and it happened when I was ending my career in the Kontinental Hockey League during the summer of 2007. I had signed with a Russian team and we were getting ready for the season by playing a handful of exhibition games. We were playing a string of five games in six nights and I found out that one of the games would be taking place in Finland.

I called Kipper to tell him I would be in Tampere, Finland, for an exhibition game and that I would love for him to come and see me. It was early August, so I was still working to get in shape and learn the European game, while Kipper had just started to get ready for his season. He was clearly still in "summer mode" when I called him and he said he'd enjoy seeing me play. In fact, Tampere was the hometown of Vesa Toskala, who was one of Kipper's best friends.

But when we got to Tampere, I was disappointed to find out I would not be starting in goal. I had played the first four games of this exhibition swing and the coach figured it would be a good time to give me a day off. Sure enough, Kipper and Vesa showed up at the start of the game, sitting in a luxury box with some of their good friends. Once they noticed I wasn't playing, they started getting restless. They started a "We want Noodles! We want Noodles!" chant inside the arena. I'm pretty sure Kipper and Vesa had enjoyed a few beverages before starting this chant, because they were really chirping from the luxury box.

Our goalie was having a rough day and suddenly we were down 3–0 and our coach had no choice but to put me into the game. As I went onto the ice, Kipper and Vesa went crazy chanting, "Noodles! Noodles! Noodles!"

I started out playing really well, making a few key saves as soon as I entered the game. I could hear those guys yelling at me from up in the luxury box and I couldn't help but laugh underneath my mask.

They starting yelling, "Shutout! Shutout! Shutout!" breaking the unwritten rule of never mentioning the S-word while a game is going on. But these were fellow members of the goaltending union, so I suppose this was acceptable.

With each passing save, they would yell, "Noodles—shutout! Noodles—shutout!"

But evidently, the age-old curse of saying the word "shutout" worked. The wheels fell off for me, as I allowed a few goals right after that and we ended up getting drubbed. All of the chanting from the luxury box stopped after those goals were scored against me.

After the game, we met up and Kipper was laughing about them acting up in the luxury box. They repaid me for their verbal abuse by taking me out for a great night in Tampere. I always teased Kipper that I was going to yell "Shutout!" to him from the press box when I was coaching him the next year.

But the funny thing is that he is not superstitious and knowing Kipper and his laid-back demeanor, it wouldn't bother him in the least. In fact, he'd probably ignore me and pass the time thinking about how he could bug Depo about Lightning, the one-eyed guinea pig.

3

Pronger, Iginla and My Favorite Teammates

Everybody always wants to know what Chris Pronger is really like away from the rink. On the ice, he has the reputation of being one of the meanest and nastiest players to ever play the game. And he tends to be short and curt when dealing with the media, so a lot of people don't know what Chris is really like when you take him away from the spotlight.

I was a teammate of his for several seasons in St. Louis and from there, we have forged a very strong friendship. I consider myself very lucky to be part of his inner circle; somebody who gets to see the real Chris Pronger on a regular basis.

Pronger is a lot like Brett Hull, in that he is an honest straight-shooter who likes to speak his mind. I've been at restaurants with him when a fan will come up to him and ask for an autograph. The exchange will usually go something like this.

Chris will be about to put some food in his mouth when a complete stranger will grab his arm.

"Excuse me, I'm really sorry and I don't mean to interrupt your meal, but I was wondering if you could sign my hat?" the fan will ask.

Chris will very bluntly reply, "You can see I'm eating my meal and you know you're interrupting me. If you can wait until we're finished here, I would be happy to sign anything for you."

That's just how he is. Chris doesn't sugarcoat anything or fluff things up, he prefers to be brutally honest. While some people might perceive that to be arrogance, I can honestly say that Chris is the furthest thing from a jerk. He treats his closest family, friends and teammates with so much respect and generosity, it's unbelievable.

When we were teammates, we would often get take-out food from this place called Crazy Bowls and Wraps in St. Louis. We would pick up meals from this place before getting on our charter plane because it was right around the corner from where we lived.

Chris used to phone me and ask me to pick up a couple of wraps and drinks for him on my way to the airport. I'd get on the plane and give him his food, but Chris would never reach into his wallet and pay me back. And this was when he was making multi-millions and I was making just above the league minimum as a backup.

It never really bothered me because eventually he would pay me back—and then some. We both used to love to talk about our favorite movies and each of us had a pretty extensive DVD collection. And sometimes I'd be sitting at home and the doorbell would ring and a FedEx man would deliver a case of 20 DVDs to my house. If you do the math—20 DVDs at $20 a pop—it more than makes up for some wraps and salads that I purchased. But Chris would never even bat an eye about this stuff; he just felt everything evened up in the end.

When I moved on from the Blues, Chris used to check in with me on a regular basis during the regular season. If we hadn't spoken in a few weeks, he would call me right out of the blue and say, "What—you win a game last week and now you're too much of a fucking big shot to call us little people back?"

And that's the real Chris Pronger—a generous, giant child who really takes care of his inner circle. I was fortunate to be there on the night that he first met his wife, Lauren, and I could tell right away they would be something special. They now have three beautiful children and the way Chris treats them is a real testament to the way he was raised himself.

He speaks to his father, Jim, his mother, Eila, and his brother, Sean, like they were all his best friends. It really is a neat family dynamic to watch. You can see how a close-knit family in Dryden,

Ontario, forged a bond that was unbreakable—even when one of the sons went on to become a multi-millionaire superstar.

But of course, in addition to the good-natured side of Chris Pronger, there is the ultimate warrior and competitor. This is the Pronger that most people are familiar with—the man who has earned a reputation of being the most physical and nasty defenseman of his generation. And I also consider myself very lucky to have seen this side of Chris from a very unique perspective.

One time, I watched Chris skate off the ice after he got cross-checked by a player from the Tampa Bay Lightning. I was sitting on the end of the bench as the backup and he clearly said to me, "I'm going to break that fucking guy's arm next time. He's dead."

I heard a lot of things while sitting on the end of the bench and, quite honestly, most of the threats never materialized. Guys love to talk trash in the heat of battle.

But, sure enough, when Chris was on the ice with the guy a few minutes later, he discreetly gave him a two-hand chop on the arm where he had no padding or protection. After the game, we found out that the Lightning player had suffered a broken wrist and was going to be sidelined for six weeks.

One of the scariest and most terrifying incidents I've ever been part of involved Chris. We were playing Detroit in the play-offs in 1998 at a time when our rivalry with them was at its peak. On May 10 that year we played in Game 2 of the series and for those of us who were inside the arena, it's a night we'll never forget. The Red Wings were winning in the third period when Boris Mironov took a slap shot from the point and Chris went to block it—even though the Wings were ahead by three or four goals at the time. As Chris blocked the shot, the puck hit him squarely in the chest, and he paused—then collapsed onto the ice.

Chris was turning blue and it looked as if he could die right on the spot. The building fell silent as the doctors and trainers from both teams came rushing onto the ice to give him emergency medical attention. Unfortunately, I had one of the best views of this whole incident, since I was sitting on the end of our bench. Chris was such a warrior that it was horrifying to see him sprawled onto the ice like that. Martin Lapointe of the Red Wings—who had been locked in a heated and intense battle with Chris all night long—skated right over to see how he was doing.

At that point, it stopped being the St. Louis Blues against the Detroit Red Wings, because the human factor kicked in. Players on both sides were genuinely concerned for Chris's health. It took all of my strength to fight back the tears, watching helplessly as they carted Chris off the ice. Nobody knew if he was dead, if he was alive or what was going to happen. I remember seeing Brett Hull also fighting the tears and talking with Steve Yzerman who had come over to the bench to see if he could do anything. The rest of that game went on, and it felt as though there wasn't another whistle, hit or shot on goal. We got drubbed by a 6–1 score, but nobody really cared about the result; we just wanted to know how our teammate and friend was doing.

The doctors said that Chris had suffered some sort of cardiac arrest when the puck hit his chest, but, miraculously, he was going to be fine. In fact, in classic Chris fashion, he convinced everybody that he was okay to play in Game 3 of that series. There are always incidents or events that make you stop and appreciate life—and I have experienced my fair share—but that was a scary moment in Detroit that made me appreciate my friendship with Chris.

The fact that Prongs played the next game was really not surprising, because when he wanted to do something, he usually did it without anybody stopping him. He will go down in history as one of the best defensemen of his generation. I was so honored to be able to play with him for a couple of seasons in St. Louis because it really gave me a terrific vantage point on how special he is.

It's no coincidence that every team he went to after the lockout—Edmonton, Anaheim and Philadelphia—all reached the Stanley Cup final in his first season with the team. He can anticipate things on the ice before they happen, which is the most valuable trait for any defenseman to have. But when you add that to his ability to position his body, his vision and his physicality, Pronger is probably the most complete defenseman to play in the NHL in the past 20 years. His offensive skills are sometimes overshadowed by everything else that he does, but ask any forward who has played with him and they'll tell you that he has the best first pass out of the zone in the game. He makes amazing stick-to-stick passes, allowing forwards to gain speed through the neutral zone. I can't tell you how many times I was thankful Chris Pronger played on my team when I was with St. Louis.

I have this distinct memory of playing a game and having a puck squirt behind me and Chris reaching out and batting the puck out of the air with his stick. It would have been a sure goal against me, but his hand-eye coordination was so amazing that he kept the puck out of my net. It's no coincidence that my GAA was always better when I played in St. Louis with Pronger. I posted a 1.95 GAA in 1999–2000 with the Blues, which just happened to be the year in which Pronger won the Hart Trophy as the MVP of the entire league. What really set Pronger apart from a Nicklas Lidstrom or Scott Niedermayer— who are also Hall of Fame defensemen—was his fire and tenacity on the ice. And it wasn't always the opposition who got the icy stares from Pronger. One night, I found out the hard way what happens when you cross Chris Pronger.

We were playing a game in Los Angeles during the 1998–99 season and it was one of the rare nights when I got the start in goal for the Blues.

Early in the first period, we were trying to kill a Kings power play and, fortunately for me, we had two of the best defensemen in the game on our team—Pronger and Al MacInnis. It was such a treat to play with these Hall of Famers, because they always told you exactly what was going on in front of you. And they had this amazing knack for knowing when to block a shot and when to step aside so you could see it clearly as a goaltender.

Chris was helping us kill this penalty and, as usual, he was yelling and talking to me all the time.

"Noodles, if you make a save, kick the rebound onto my stick and I'll clear it out," he promised.

Sure enough, the puck went to the point and one of the Kings defensemen took a shot. And it was one of these slow-motion, knuckleball shots that takes forever to get to the net. As it came toward me, Chris reminded me of the plan, tapping his stick on the ice and saying, "Noodles, put the rebound here."

Chris stepped aside so I had a clear view of the incoming shot, which was going to be a piece of cake to save. But I overplayed the rebound and this thing took off like a rocket. It went flying off my stick and instead of softly landing on Chris's stick, it ricocheted back to the other point.

And standing there, with drool coming down his mouth, was Rob Blake—who couldn't believe he was about to get a golden opportunity for a one-timer.

So Blake just absolutely blasted the puck back toward the net with one of his most powerful slap shots. As I mentioned, Chris always had a knack for knowing when to block a shot and so he decided to block this one, because this was a Grade-A scoring chance for Blake and the Kings.

But unfortunately for Chris, he blocked the shot in one of the worst possible places—the top of his foot. Despite being in a tremendous amount of pain after blocking the shot, he was able to clear the puck down the zone.

And he looked back at me and screamed, "You fucking idiot—I said put the puck on my stick!"

I was so rattled, I kept yelling, "Sorry, sorry, sorry!"

Chris hobbled off the ice and before he got back to the bench, he turned and glared at me one more time. "Wake up!" he yelled at the top of his voice. Then he walked right down the hallway to the dressing room to get medical attention.

And now my mind was racing. Did I just accidentally hurt the best defenseman in the NHL? I play a handful of games per year and I might have just contributed to the injury of our Hart Trophy candidate. This is not going to look good on my resume.

I was not looking forward to the sound of the buzzer at the end of the first period, when I would have to deal with more criticism from Chris. As I walked into the dressing room and sat down in my stall, there was a clear line of vision from my seat to the training table. Chris was sitting there and staring me down. He started pointing and yelling at me, "Fuck you!" It was clear that he was still really pissed off at me.

The medical staff had done X-rays on his foot and, fortunately, the results had come back negative. I would have been crushed if Chris had broken a bone in his foot and blamed me for the injury.

Chris did have a severe bruise on his foot, but as he usually did he went back out there and dominated the rest of the game. We ended up beating the Kings.

Finally, after the game, I was able to have a conversation with him about what had happened earlier.

"Why are you so mad at me?" I asked him.

"Dude, we're in Los Angeles. We want to go out and have some fun. And the training staff wants to put a walking boot on my foot. That's why I'm pissed off."

In the end, Chris didn't have to wear the walking boot— which would have totally cramped his style on the LA scene. But he did walk around with a huge limp all night and for a few weeks after that he kept reminding me about how sore his foot was.

Another time, I felt the wrath of Pronger in front of my family and friends. We were playing a road game in Edmonton and Joel Quenneville decided to give me the start since he knew it would be a special night.

In the first period, Chris was in our zone with the puck, trying to execute a breakout play. The goalies had a simple way of communicating with our defensemen when we were in St. Louis. When a player was chasing one of our guys, we just yelled out, "Man on!" But if someone had our defenseman lined up for a hit, we would scream, "Heads up!" We could be a second set of eyes for our defensemen and warn them of an impending hit.

During this particular breakout play, I was yelling, "Man on, Man on!" because there was a forechecker chasing Pronger. However, I neglected to see Ethan Moreau coming into the picture and he made a beeline for Pronger from his blind side.

Moreau absolutely crushed Pronger in the center of the ice, flattening him with a hit that Pronger usually dished out to opponents. I realized that I was going to be wearing the goat horns on this one, too, since I failed to warn him about Ethan Moreau.

During the TV timeout, I made sure I didn't go over to the defensemen's side of the bench, because I wanted to avoid Pronger. But he was yelling at me from his side, "Don't you know our fucking wording on the ice?"

It was so obvious that he was yelling at me that my brother Dave even asked me about it after the game. From his seat up in the stands, he could tell that Pronger was fuming at me—that's how intense he was on the ice. I've never played with such a perfectionist or someone who demanded so much out of his teammates. Chris Pronger made us all better players and that's why every team he played for seemed to reach the Stanley Cup final.

One of my other favorite stories with Chris happened the next season, when we had a few nights off at home in St. Louis during the regular season. We decided to go out and have a big night on the town, because we didn't play again for four nights.

Chris, Jamal Mayers and I were going to meet up with Mark McGwire for a fun evening. This was pretty cool company for Jamal and myself to be hanging with—the reigning MVP of the NHL and the home-run king in baseball.

Mark actually had a baseball game that night at Busch Stadium, so the three of us went to a bar to wait for him to join us. We found a table with a view of the Cardinals game so we could keep an eye on how Mark was doing. Suddenly, Chris's cell phone rings and it's Mark, calling him from the dugout.

"I've got one more at-bat and then I'm out of here. I'll be there in twenty minutes," McGwire told Chris.

I can't imagine using a cell phone to phone somebody from the end of the bench in the middle of a hockey game, but I suppose the rules are a little more lax in baseball. Come to think of it, whatever rules were in place probably didn't apply to Mark McGwire anyway.

And just like he promised, Mark walked into the bar and joined us about 20 minutes later. He had to bring some security guys with him, because at that point he was still the most recognizable player in baseball.

We had a great dinner, hit a few bars and then ended up going across the river to this bar called Pops, a place where we used to go quite a bit. In fact, I would often get up on stage and play drums with the house band.

The drinks were flowing and we were having a great time—especially because in the back of our minds, we knew we didn't have to play a game for another four days. We did have practice in the morning around 11, but we were veterans who knew how to get through a skate with a hangover.

The night just flew by, past midnight and the wee hours of the morning. It was around 6 a.m. when one of us remembered that we had a mandatory team breakfast to attend at 7:30 a.m. This was one of those corporate breakfasts where our season ticket holders and sponsors paid large amounts of money to sit at a table with the players.

Needless to say, we were a little bit panicked at that point. I ended up sleeping for about 30 minutes back at my apartment and Chris also grabbed a quick nap at his place for about 45 minutes and then we had to grab a cab and head down to the event. We were still pretty hammered and the last thing we wanted to do was interact with our most valuable customers over a formal breakfast.

But I really lucked out on that particular morning. When I walked into the room, I found out I was totally off the hook: The people who had paid to sit at my table hadn't shown up for some reason. I didn't have to make small talk with these corporate folks and season ticket holders while I was totally out to lunch.

For Chris, however, it was a different story. Not only was his table packed with fans, but he was expected to get up at the podium and make a speech to the entire audience since he was the captain of the team and the reigning Hart Trophy winner.

I once again got one of those classic Chris Pronger icy stares, as he was pissed off that he had to make a speech while I was just sitting there at an empty table. There probably haven't been a lot of instances when Chris Pronger has wanted to trade lives with Jamie McLennan, but I'm pretty sure that was one of them.

Chris walked up to the podium to make his speech in front of hundreds of people. (And when I say "walked," I mean "staggered.") His speech was clearly disjointed and rambling, because not only was he unprepared—he was still lathered.

"Umm . . . I'd like to, uh . . . thank everyone . . . for uh . . . coming out here this morning. This is . . . uh . . . a great event," he said awkwardly.

He was butchering this speech so badly that he desperately needed to be saved. And Joel Quenneville—being the great coach that he was—jumped right up on stage and took over the microphone.

"Thanks for those words, Chris. Now go grab a seat," Quenneville said.

As the breakfast was wrapping up, we figured we had a couple of hours to try to grab some sleep before practice started. But Quenneville went up to a few guys and said that he wanted to work on the power play a little bit early. Chris, being the point man on the power play, had to go out an hour early. I was chuckling at Chris's misfortunes—until Coach Q found me.

"Noodles, we need you on the ice with the power play unit."

I had no choice but to accept the coach's request, but this was going to be difficult. I was still so bombed that I'd probably be seeing at least two pucks every time somebody took a shot at me.

We got on the ice and Chris and I were exchanging glances with each other. We just wanted to get through this practice and then find a place to sleep it off.

The worst part about being a goalie for the power play drills is that it's often a five-on-zero situation. There are no defensemen or penalty killers to help me out. So these guys are just teeing up and firing pucks at me from all angles. Trying to stop an Al MacInnis slap shot when I was stone-cold sober was one of the most difficult things to do as a goalie. Just imagine how much fun it would be to try it when you're totally smashed.

Not a word of a lie, I did not make a single save that day. Usually, you make a save or two just by sheer accident—but not on that day. The only puck that did not go into the net was a shot from the point that sailed high over the glass behind me. And of course that shot was taken by the equally inebriated Chris Pronger.

At the end of the power play practice, the other players started to come onto the ice for the 11 a.m. full-team skate. We were all skating around the rink for warm-up when Quenneville pulled me and Chris over to the side for a little chat.

When you're clearly dogging it on the ice and the coach wants to have a word with you, there is a little sense of fear that enters your body. The last thing you want to do is have your coach question your work ethic and dedication. So Chris and I were prepared for a tongue-lashing from Quenneville.

"Hey, where was the party last night—and why wasn't I invited?" Quenneville said with a sly grin.

The three of us all started laughing.

"Just have a good practice and get some rest," Quenneville said as he skated away.

But I wasn't out of the woods just yet. The rest of the guys on the team had heard about our antics and made sure it was going to be a rough practice. Geoff Courtnall and Marc Bergevin took slap shots and were trying to hit me in the groin throughout the whole practice because they wanted to see me throw up.

It was probably the hardest practice I ever had as an NHL goalie. But considering I got the chance to hang out with Prongs and Big Mac the night before, I would say it was something I would do all over again.

The Day Jarome Iginla Wore His Own Jersey in Public to See if Anyone Would Notice

Hockey fans and insiders know Jarome Iginla as one of the most fierce and intense competitors of his generation. And when he scored his 500th career goal, it also cemented his status as one of the best goal-scorers in hockey history. But I simply know Jarome Iginla as "Iggy," a person I'm also fortunate to have in my inner circle and one of the best friends I've ever had in my life.

In a lot of ways, the Jarome Iginla you see on the ice isn't all that different from the Iggy I see behind closed doors in social situations. When we have poker night at his house in Calgary, Iggy is just as intense and competitive as he would be during a regular season game against the Oilers. Iggy basically *has* to win—or else the game just keeps on going. If he folds in a game of poker and everybody is ready to go to sleep, you can be sure that we're going to play another round until Iggy wins.

And this unbridled passion for victory extends to board games, where Iggy's desire to win is legendary in our circle of friends. We used to have Risk night at his place and things would never be over until Iggy ruled the world. If someone happened to knock off Iggy's army in Europe, he would badger the other players until they allowed him back into the game. Iggy's approach could be stated simply: "You guys are at my house playing Risk, so if I'm eliminated from the game, you can go find another place to play."

When you see that type of desire and intensity in a board game, it gives you a pretty good understanding of why Iggy is one of the best power forwards in the history of the NHL. How many players in the history of the NHL could score, hit and fight like Jarome Iginla? The guy just never quits until he gets what he wants—and that's exactly the type of trait you want to have in your captain.

The thing about Iggy is that in addition to being a ferocious competitor, he is also one of the funnier people around. His sense of humor probably doesn't come through during those TV interviews you see with him, because he's forced to speak in clichés.

And while there is a phrase that "what happens in Vegas, stays in Vegas," I have to tell one story about Iggy's bachelor party weekend that illustrates how funny he can be with his friends.

Every summer a bunch of us—me, Iggy, Jason Strudwick, Tyson Nash, Jason Holland and several others—plan a boys' trip somewhere in North America. When it was Iggy's bachelor party weekend, I was in charge of planning a lot of the festivities. We decided to spend two days in Los Angeles, followed by two days in Las Vegas.

When we were in Vegas, we decided to spend some time next to the pool in our hotel. One of Iggy's best friends, a guy named Bill, had come along on the trip with us and he had brought some Flames memorabilia that he wanted to get signed. Included in Bill's collection was a replica Jarome Iginla Calgary Flames jersey. Just before we left our room to head down to the pool, Iggy had a brilliant idea.

"Hey, guys, I bet I could wear my own jersey down to the pool and nobody would recognize me," he said.

Bill and I looked at each other in disbelief. Jarome Iginla wanted to wear his own jersey in public to see if he would be recognized? This would never happen in Calgary, where Iggy would probably be spotted if he were wearing a trench coat and sunglasses. But here in Vegas, Iggy was feeling adventurous.

So Bill and I set the ground rules for this little dare and decided that Iggy would have to walk one lap around the pool wearing his own #12 Calgary Flames jersey.

We all headed down to the pool area wearing our big, fluffy, white hotel robes. But as soon as we got to the pool, Iggy dropped his robe to reveal his jersey.

The pool area was packed with people, because it was a hot summer day in Vegas. As Iggy started his walk around the pool, nobody seemed to notice. After all, it's fairly common practice for fans to wear jerseys of their favorite players or teams while they're on vacation. But I can't think of another time when a superstar athlete wore his own jersey out in public just to see if anyone would notice.

Iggy wasn't allowed to run around the pool, so he kept a fairly slow and methodical pace as he paraded himself around the hotel pool. Our whole group was howling with laughter in the corner, because we couldn't believe how awesome this looked. A stunt like this could never work in Canada and yet it was unfolding in front of our eyes in the Las Vegas sun.

Just as he was about to complete his lap around the pool undetected, a gentleman sat up from his poolside chair and called out to him.

"Hey, man, you actually look a lot like Jarome Iginla."

Iggy just sort of half-acknowledged him and kept walking along. When he got back to our area, he pulled off his Iginla sweater and rolled it up into a bag like it was nothing. But we were in hysterics because Iggy had just completed one full lap and the boys were loving it.

Because of his sense of humor, Iggy has been able to stay very grounded, level and humble. The guy pretty much radiates a positive vibe and energy, no matter what the circumstance. One time, Iggy was mired in a terrible slump—he hadn't scored a goal in seven or eight games. The media in Calgary was all over him, scrutinizing his every shift during the slump. I figured this stuff would be weighing him down because nobody wants to see their face on the front page of the sports section with a negative headline. We had a great one-on-one conversation inside the Flames dressing room because I was concerned about how Iggy was doing mentally, given the pressure and burden that was on him to score a goal.

"Iggy, how's it going? How are you feeling?" I asked him.

"You know what, Noodles? I'm all right. But I can't wait to get scoring again. I can feel it coming, bud."

And that was Iggy in a nutshell. Instead of being worn down by the negativity surrounding him, he chose to focus on the positive feeling of scoring his next goal. And he had such confidence in his ability that he knew another goal was just around the corner.

A player with his resume could easily be forgiven if he remained aloof from his fans and the public. But that's just not in his makeup. There were countless times when we were out in public and some fans came up to Iggy and just wanted to talk to him. He would always stop and chat with these fans, sign autographs and take pictures. So many times I would be like, "Come on, Iggy—it's time to get out of here." And I would literally have to pry him out of the restaurant because he was engaged in a conversation with fans.

Iggy always tries to remember the name of any person he's just met. You can see that he relates to people on a personal level and it's truly amazing to watch how he deals with fans.

The most infamous story about Iggy and his generosity toward fans came during the Winter Olympics in Salt Lake City in 2002. If you recall, it was sort of Jarome Iginla's coming-out party on the global stage. That NHL season was his breakout campaign, where he scored 50 goals for the first time and surprised a lot of people by making it onto the Canadian Olympic hockey team.

While he was down in Salt Lake City, Iggy went for dinner one day with his family outside of the Olympic village. Seated next to them was a table of fans from Calgary, who had driven down to cheer on Team Canada. True to form, Iggy struck up a lengthy conversation with these fans. It turns out the four guys had driven all the way down from Calgary just to be around the Olympic atmosphere. They didn't have tickets to any of the events; in fact they didn't even have a hotel room. They were sleeping in their car, but they just wanted to soak in some of the atmosphere. And having just met their idol, Jarome Iginla, it made the whole trip worthwhile.

Once Iggy heard about their story, he excused himself from the table. A few minutes later he came back and announced that he had booked a hotel room for these guys in Salt Lake City. He took one of their cell phone numbers and told them he would be in touch with them at some point during the Olympics. What these four fans didn't know is that Iggy was putting the wheels in motion to get these guys tickets to a Team Canada hockey game. A couple of days later, these guys received a phone call from a Hockey Canada representative saying that Jarome Iginla had arranged four tickets to a game for them.

It was the kind of story that was almost too far-fetched to believe. An NHL superstar runs into four fans, books them a hotel and arranges tickets to an Olympic hockey game for them? Iggy wanted to keep the story quiet, but of course these four fans wanted the world to know how generous Jarome Iginla had been to them. So as soon as they got back to Alberta, they phoned the newspapers and radio stations and, pretty soon, everybody heard about this story.

I can tell you that Iggy does stuff like this all the time, but it doesn't always make it into the media. I've never been around a more generous and gracious athlete in my life. And I'm not talking about being gracious with his money—although he is. But it's the time he spends getting to know people that really makes Jarome Iginla a special person.

So far I've relayed stories about how fierce, competitive, humorous and generous Iggy can be when you get to know him. But I'd like to end this section with a story about his stubbornness. After all, I think I need to debunk the theory that Jarome Iginla is a saint who can do no wrong.

During my first week as an assistant coach with the Flames, Iggy and I were involved in a little on-ice incident that remains a bone of contention between us.

Midway through a practice drill on the ice, Iggy shot the puck hard into the offensive zone. But the puck ricocheted off a seam in the glass and headed right toward me. I put my hands up to protect my face, but at the last second, the puck hit me in the head. Since I was an assistant coach, I wasn't wearing a helmet at the time and it really stung me.

"Hey, you just hit me in the head with the puck!" I yelled at him.

"What are you talking about? No, I didn't," he responded.

"Iggy, I just watched you dump the puck into the zone and it hit the glass and then it hit me in the head."

"Well, that wasn't me who shot the puck. And besides, you didn't get hit in the head."

Now Iggy was skeptical that I even got hit with the puck. So I turned and showed him where the blood was trickling down the side of my face. But he still didn't own up to it.

I skated off the ice to get medical attention and was chirping Iggy the whole way. I ended up getting six stitches on my forehead from our team doctor thanks to him.

Of all the souvenirs I've received from Iggy over the years, I am least grateful for that one.

Wendel Clark Shows Off His Toughness and Leadership

When people think about Wendel Clark's career, they automatically picture him wearing a Toronto Maple Leafs jersey. After all, for almost a decade, Wendel had blue and white coursing through his veins and he was one of the most popular sports figures in the history of Toronto.

I was fortunate enough to play one season with Wendel with the New York Islanders in 1995–96. We had a very odd mix of players on that team and we were like a franchise with no clear direction. We had some really good young players like Ziggy Palffy, Todd Bertuzzi and Bryan McCabe. But we also had a collection of veterans, including Wendel, Pat Flatley and Derek King, who wanted to win right away. We had Mike Milbury running our team as the head coach and we finished in last place with just 54 points.

Having Mike as a head coach was a unique experience because he often had some very strange ideas about how to play the game and how he should motivate his players. And that would sometimes clash directly with a guy like Wendel, who was a no-nonsense person both on and off the ice.

One night during that 1995–96 season, we were in Los Angeles to play the Kings when they still had Wayne Gretzky. Before the game, Mike went on and on about how we had to contain Gretzky—which wasn't exactly breaking news to any of us inside the locker room.

"We can't give Gretzky any time and space. We have to close on him quickly," Mike said to us in his pre-game speech. "Make sure you are on him at all times." In theory, this was a great idea because we needed to focus on Gretzky. But the problem was, Gretzky had made a living out of being the best passer in the game for the past 15 years and nobody could really stop him. So if all our defenders would swarm at him, he would easily find an outlet to make a pass to set somebody up for a scoring chance. In hindsight, we should have made sure that we covered all of his passing options and forced Gretzky to play to the outside.

But Mike was adamant, as we hit the ice in Los Angeles, that our defenders should all go to Gretzky. Sure enough, in the first shift of the game, Gretzky had the puck entering our zone. And about three of our players decided to go right at him, making sure they were following Mike's pre-game plan.

Gretzky didn't panic. He simply flipped a nice saucer pass over to Dmitri Khristich who came in and beat me on a breakaway.

A couple of minutes later, we tried the same thing on Gretzky and he set up another goal. And by the halfway mark of the first period, Gretzky had three assists and Mike gave me the hook from the net because were losing 3–0. From the end of the bench I had a terrific perspective of the rest of the game as Gretzky continued to torch us. Mike's pre-game plan was a complete failure, but he kept pressing guys to go after Gretzky. As the final buzzer sounded, we had lost 9–2, with Tommy Soderstrom as my replacement for the final six goals that Los Angeles scored. And that Gretzky guy we tried to contain ended up with six points—one goal and five assists.

What I remember most about that game is Wendel Clark's unbelievable passion—even during a blowout loss. In that game against the Kings, Wendel had two of the best fights I've ever witnessed in my career. Both of them were against Marty McSorley, who was considered one of the true heavyweights of his era. And while Wendel gave up a lot of size and weight to Marty, he stood in and went toe-to-toe with Marty in those two fights. They had had a memorable fight during the conference final three years earlier, when Wendel was still in Toronto, so maybe these two fights were a carryover from that unforgettable bout.

In any event, it showed how passionate Wendel Clark was as a hockey player. And after the game—when we had been humiliated and embarrassed by the Kings—it wasn't our head coach who came in and delivered the memorable speech to our troops. (After all, Mike probably didn't have much to say, since his pre-game plan of stopping Gretzky was a complete failure.) It was Wendel who stood up in the room and started talking. And because Wendel didn't often speak his mind inside the dressing room, we all took notice.

Wendel's message was direct and blunt. "We're fooling ourselves if we don't think we need our best effort every night—just to be a good team." And he was absolutely right. No amount of pre-game scheming from Mike Milbury was going to compensate for our lack of talent. We weren't an elite team and Wendel was reminding us of that. And because he had just fought Marty McSorley twice, and was speaking to us now with his knuckles bloody and swollen, Wendel had more credibility inside our dressing room.

I remember another moment in the dressing room, a few weeks later, when Wendel once again showed his passion and intensity for the game.

We were about to have a skate at our practice facility in Long Island and Mike came into the room and started criticizing the players individually. This is something that a lot of coaches will do to try and motivate players during the course of a long season. While one-on-one meetings are sometimes effective, coaches also find it useful to criticize you in front of your peers—so you feel a little bit embarrassed. On this particular day, Mike was going around the room and chirping at different guys. He came to me and said, "McLennan—we need you to be sharper out there. You gotta stop the pucks."

"Hey, Ziggy, remember we're paying you to score goals, right?"

Then it was Wendel's turn to face the heat. But Mike had to be cautious when going after Wendel, since he was one of the few players who was actually in the league when Mike himself was a player. Wendel was the type of player who carried a lot of respect inside the dressing room and chances are he would not enjoy being verbally challenged by the head coach.

"Wendel, I brought you in here to be a leader and to be engaged with these guys. And you don't talk to anybody. You're in the fucking back room stretching by yourself instead of talking to the kids and helping them to get better," Mike said.

Now just for a little background information here, Wendel suffered from severe back pain in the latter stages of his career. Before every game, he'd go to the back area or the training room and do a whole series of stretches to try to loosen up his back. He wasn't trying to be antisocial or to shirk his leadership role, he was just trying to get his back in a state where he felt comfortable enough to play.

Wendel was none too pleased to be challenged by Milbury in front of the entire team, so he stood up and went right back at Mike verbally. I forget exactly what was said, but I remember being impressed at Wendel's ability and leadership to stand up for himself and the team. Most of us just took Mike's criticism without saying anything in return, but Wendel defended himself and the team and went right back at Milbury.

Mike was genuinely surprised at Wendel's emotional reaction, but he tried to act as if this was all part of a premeditated strategy of his.

He looked at all of us and said, "Now that's the type of intensity I'd like to see you all play with every night."

With that, he walked out of the room.

Wendel Clark may have had a bad back, and he may have been forced to play on a directionless New York Islanders team, but nothing could stop him from bringing passion and fire to the rink every day.

The Real Scoop on Nicknames Inside the Dressing Room

When you watch a player being interviewed on television after a game, he will usually refer to his teammates by a nickname. For example, if someone is asking Jonathan Toews about Patrick Kane, he might say, "Kaner was great for us tonight."

Nicknames for hockey players these days are criticized for being too boring. Daniel Alfredsson is simply "Alfie," while Mike Richards is "Richie." The creativity for nicknames has seemingly gone out the window, as the days of "The Flower," "The Golden Jet" and "The Russian Rocket" seem to be long gone.

Inside the dressing room, however, the tradition of giving unique nicknames is alive and well. It's just that you won't hear these ones on television because players love to have their own little insider nicknames for their teammates. Here are some of my favorites from over the years:

"Lemon Juice" was our nickname for Lubomir Sekeras, whom I played with in Minnesota. He was a great guy, but he always looked like he was sucking on a lemon.

Roman Hamrlik was called "Carpie" when we played together in Calgary. He made the mistake of telling me and Kipper one day about the Czech tradition of keeping a live carp in your bathtub for the month of December, until it was cooked at Christmas. We totally abused him for sharing a tub with a carp.

"Fred Flintstone": All you need to do is Google an image of Sean O'Donnell and you'll know why we gave him this cartoon nickname.

"Hobby Horse": When I played with Jozef Stumpel in Florida, we used to tease him that he had wooden legs because he never bent them.

Because he had a long chin that looked like a horse, we used to call Jeff Finley "Trigger" inside the dressing room.

Mike Eastwood used to slink around and have a mysterious aura about him, so we referred to him as "Darkman" in St. Louis.

"Helmut Balderis": This was our nickname for Robert Petrovicky because he had a really big head. Robert always said, "Hey guys, I don't like being called that." So naturally, guys would call him that even more.

"Ugger" was a short form for "ugly," our name for Darius Kasparaitis. But he was also one of the best guys inside the dressing room, with a great personality, so this was almost a term of endearment for him.

4

Al Arbour and the Brain-teaser

By the time I had my first training camp with the New York Islanders, the glory days of the franchise were long gone.

The likes of Denis Potvin, Mike Bossy, Billy Smith and Bryan Trottier had either retired or moved on to different organizations. The club that had captured four Stanley Cups in a row in the early 1980s had become, just 10 short years later, the laughingstock of the Patrick Division.

However, there was one holdover from the Islanders dynasty who served as a transition to the newcomers like me. His name was Al Arbour.

From a statistical standpoint, Arbour is one of the greatest coaches in the history of the National Hockey League. In wins and games coached, he ranks second only to Scotty Bowman, and he spent a remarkable 1,500 games behind the bench for the Islanders franchise alone. (It should also be pointed out that Arbour actually beat Bowman in their last head-to-head play-off meeting—when our 1993 Islanders stunned the two-time defending Cup champion Penguins.)

But, as with all great coaches, the story of Al Arbour goes far beyond the impressive statistics.

I found this out during my first exhibition game with the Islanders back in 1991. I had been drafted by the club earlier that summer and was eagerly anticipating my first taste of real NHL action. I knew it was likely to come during a pre-season game in September and sure enough, Al Arbour tabbed me as the starter for a game against Boston.

The exhibition game against the Bruins was actually taking place in Albany, New York, but for me it carried all the importance of a game being played at the Boston Garden or Nassau Coliseum. I was really hoping to showcase my abilities to Arbour and the rest of the Islanders brass.

I figured that an exhibition game would be a nice way to ease into the NHL. There was a good chance that the Bruins would not be icing their A-lineup, since these pre-season games were often used to examine the progress of rookies and prospects. And I was relieved to know that Cam Neely would not be playing, since he was still sidelined by the injury he'd suffered from an Ulf Samuelsson hit in the playoffs a few months earlier.

But for some reason, Rick Bowness decided that it was a good night to start the rest of his veteran squad against us. So the Bruins lineup featured the likes of Raymond Bourque, Glen Wesley, Craig Janney and Vladimir Ruzicka. Al Arbour countered with a lineup that looked a lot like our projected AHL squad, so this was a complete mismatch from the start.

A couple of minutes into the game, the Bruins connected for their first goal. And then, a minute later, they scored again. I mean, Bourque and Wesley were just teeing up shots from the point and I felt like I had no chance. The game was not even 10 minutes old and the Bruins had jumped out to a 4–0 lead. This was certainly not the way I had envisioned my first game in the NHL.

As soon as the Bruins scored the fourth goal, Arbour called a timeout and signaled me to the bench. I figured I might be getting the hook from the coach after embarrassing myself in such a short time. I skated over to the bench, fully expecting to receive the wrath from a Hall of Fame coach.

Arbour yelled at me, "Hey, kid. If I flipped your net over and put a bird inside, would you be able to keep it in there?"

I was completely taken aback. Here I was, 20 years old and in my first NHL game, and I was being given a strange brain-teaser by a coaching legend during a timeout.

"What???" I replied, in a voice of utter disbelief. I was sure I had misheard his question. There was no way he had just asked me about trapping a live bird inside my net, right?

But Arbour simply restated the original question.

"I said, if I flipped your net over and put a bird inside, would you be able to keep it in there?"

I gave him a blank stare, as I was unsure of how to answer this riddle. Before I could stumble and bumble my way through a response, Arbour pointed for me to go back into the net.

As I skated back to my crease, I had completely forgotten about allowing those four goals in the first 10 minutes of the game. I was now wondering what this bird comment meant from Al Arbour. Our team was able to respond with the next goal and as the game progressed, we cut the gap. The Bruins scored one more goal against me, but we rallied late in the game and managed to salvage a 5–5 tie. After Arbour's peculiar bird comment to me, we outscored the Boston Bruins 5–1.

Following the game, I was eager to find out exactly what the coach meant by his question. I couldn't wait to hear the deep meaning behind this analogy. I wondered if this was some sort of secret question that he used to enlighten Billy Smith back in the day. I approached Arbour in the dressing room.

"Hey, coach, I still can't figure out that riddle. What did all that bird stuff mean?"

Arbour looked at me and said wryly, "It doesn't mean any-thing at all. You looked so rattled out there that I had to get you to come to the bench and change your train of thought."

It was as simple as that. There was no bird metaphor; no deeper meaning to Arbour's bizarre bird question. He just saw a 20-year-old kid looking like a deer in headlights and he wanted to help him out. And rather than chew me out in front of my entire team, he decided to take a very unorthodox approach.

At that point, I understood how special it was going to be to have Al Arbour behind the bench. Al was amazing because he was a player's coach without being inside our dressing room too much. He was able to take the pulse of our room and yet he hardly ever set foot on our turf. And when he did cross paths with us, he almost always left a positive impression.

One night in my rookie season on Long Island, we were playing an important home game in April. We were right on the playoff bubble and there were significant playoff implica-tions on the line. I was backing up Ron Hextall that night, so as usual I was pretty relaxed knowing that I probably wasn't going to see any game action.

During the first intermission, I decided to go into the play-ers' lounge just outside our dressing room. When I wasn't play-ing, I didn't mind popping into that room to see what was on television. I walked into the lounge and Steve Thomas, Ray Ferraro and Derek King were all sitting there, watching golf on the big screen. I knew it was the Masters Tournament, but I was thinking this probably wasn't the ideal time for our three best offensive players to be watching golf. We were in the middle of a do-or-die game and these guys were watching golf when they should probably have been diagramming a new wrinkle to the power play.

Right on cue, Al Arbour walked into the room. I sort of slid back and waited for him to start cursing at his trio of stars.

Instead, Al looked up at the screen and said, "What's Fuzzy shooting?"

I was flabbergasted. Instead of chewing out the players for a lack of focus, he engaged them in a two-minute discussion about golf. They chatted about Fuzzy Zoeller's day and then Al simply walked out of the room.

It was bizarre to see a Hall of Fame coach with the ability to relate to his players like that. It was like nothing ever fazed Al Arbour. He lost his cool with us at certain times, but that was only because he knew exactly what buttons he could push. Most of the time, he knew that players needed to be treated like men. There was no point in being a tyrant because players don't respond well to a dictatorship. For the record, we ended up making the playoffs that year.

Trying to Count Darryl Sutter's Swearwords

The HBO series *24/7* has given hockey fans a terrific behind-the-scenes view of life in the National Hockey League.

For those of us who've been fortunate enough to play in the league, the series does not offer too many surprises—especially when it comes to the vulgar language. A lot of fans were shocked to hear how many F-bombs were dropped by Bruce Boudreau when the HBO cameras were following him as head coach of the Washington Capitals. But I wasn't fazed in the least bit because I had played for Darryl Sutter with the Calgary Flames, who could make some of Bruce Boudreau's speeches sound like they belonged at a church picnic.

I distinctly remember sitting one time with our goalie coach, Dave Marcoux, and making a bet with him before one of Darryl's pre-game speeches to the team.

"I wonder how many times Darryl will say 'fuck' during this speech," I said. I wasn't sure how many times he could say the word, but Darryl would say "fuck" more often than any other word in the English language. Dave agreed to keep track during this particular speech. I was thinking he'd count at least 20 or 30 of them.

So Darryl gets into the room and starts his speech. "Fuck. We have to fucking work harder. Fuck me. What the fuck? It's not that fucking difficult for fuck's sake. Just wake the fuck up."

No word of a lie, in Darryl's two-minute speech to the team that day, Dave Marcoux counted 63 different uses of the word "fuck." It's something we still laugh about to this day because I never thought someone could use any word—let alone "fuck"—63 different times in the span of two minutes.

That's a "fuck" every 1.90 seconds for those of you who enjoy the mathematics behind the swearing.

But Darryl's 63-fuck speech was not his most memorable one as coach of the Calgary Flames. That distinction came on October 25, 2003. We had lost at home to the St. Louis Blues 2–1 the night before in a pretty lifeless game for each team. St. Louis only took one penalty the whole night and we did not engage with them physically. We had to turn around the next night and play up the road in Edmonton, a Saturday night game on *Hockey Night in Canada*.

Darryl did not want his team to be embarrassed, so we expected a tongue-lashing from him prior to the morning skate. We were all sitting around in our full gear inside the visitors' dressing room at Rexall Place when Darryl walked into the room. He was still fuming about the loss on home ice to St. Louis the night before; you could see the smoke still coming out of his ears.

Our video coach, Rob Cookson, had set up a television in the middle of the dressing room, so we also knew there would be video evidence of our shortcomings against St. Louis.

The first words out of Darryl's mouth were, "Guys, what was on the board last night before the game against St. Louis?"

Prior to every game, Darryl would write some key points on the whiteboard before we played an opponent. They would usually contain information about the team we were playing and what we needed to do to win the game. Clearly, we hadn't paid attention to Darryl's whiteboard message the night before.

"Come on, guys, what was on the board last night?" he asked again.

One of the guys replied, "'Have a good start.'"

"That's right. Have a good fucking start. Cookie, roll the video."

So Rob Cookson hit the play button and it was the opening face-off from last night's game against the Blues. Ten seconds into the game, Dean McAmmond got absolutely crushed by St. Louis forward Jamal Mayers.

"Stop the tape right there," barked Sutter. "Dean McAmmond—you didn't come to play last night. And that's what you get—you get fucking hurt. Now roll the tape again."

The video continued to play and it showed McAmmond lying on the ice and Chris Clark coming over to see what had happened. Sutter stopped the tape again and now started berating Clark for his lack of response to Jamal Mayers.

"What are you going to do there, Clarkie—are you going to fucking give Jamal Mayers a kiss? You're not going to fight him. Jamal Mayers—you're afraid of him, Clarkie. You fucking warrior."

And then we realized what was going to happen on this morning. This was not a garden variety pre-game speech where the coach was angry at you and asked everybody to play better. Darryl Sutter was going to go around the room and rip each and every player in the room for last night's game against St. Louis. You could feel each guy start to slink down in his locker stall, knowing his turn was coming next. I can guarantee that each guy in the room was thinking, "Oh god—what video evidence does he have against me?"

For the next 30 minutes, Darryl Sutter went around that room and buried every player on the team. And he kept referencing that whiteboard message from the night before.

"Guys, what else was on that list? Don't give up a power play goal to the Blues, right? Cookie, roll the fucking tape again."

And sure enough, it's a video clip of Doug Weight scoring a power play goal against us. And this time, Toni Lydman was the one wearing the goat horns.

"Toni Lydman, you're playing like a fucking broad!" Darryl yelled. "You've been asleep for the past six weeks— why don't you just fucking go back to sleep right now? Fuck off, Toni."

And he just kept going around the room like that.

"Oleg Saprykin, you've got your fucking white skates on. You're like a soccer player out there—'Don't hit me, don't hit me!' I can't believe we pay you a million dollars because you're a product of this system," he barked. "A million fucking dollars? You're a waste of money!"

"But don't worry, Oleg, Chris Clark will protect you because he's a warrior."

Nobody was safe from Darryl's wrath on this day. Even Jarome Iginla heard it from the coach in front of everyone.

"Jarome Iginla, what are you going to do tonight in front of your hometown crowd? Are you going to play hard or are you going to kiss Ryan Smyth out there?"

Darryl saved his best verbal barrage for Krzysztof Oliwa. For those who may not remember Oliwa, he was a resident tough guy who racked up almost 1,500 penalty minutes in a short career in the NHL.

"Krzysztof Oliwa—why did I sign you? Our team hasn't had a fighting major all season. You're trying to be a fancy player out there instead of just playing tough. I'll put you in the stands if you don't want to stick up for your teammates. Are you going to be afraid of Georges Laraque tonight? You're useless to this team unless you stick up for your teammates."

I was fortunate enough to avoid the wrath of Darryl on this day. It wasn't that he didn't have any ammunition to use against me. After all, I had been the losing goalie in the game against St. Louis the night before. But since Roman Turek was out with a knee injury, I was Darryl's only legitimate option to play in goal against Edmonton. If he verbally abused me a few hours before the Oilers game, there was no telling what psychological damage he could do to his goalie. There are times when it pays to be thought of as an emotionally fragile, stand-in starting goalie in the NHL—and this was definitely one of them.

So whenever Darryl looked in my direction, he just skipped over me and went on to the next player. Finally, the half-hour hate-fest ended with these words from Darryl Sutter: "You guys can go out there and skate this morning or you can do fuck all. It doesn't really matter. Edmonton will skate all over you guys tonight if you're not ready."

And with that, Darryl Sutter walked out of the room and left us in a state of stunned disbelief.

This was going to go one of two ways in Edmonton: Either we were going to hit the ice as an inspired team to prove Darryl Sutter wrong—or we were going to just quit on the head coach. There was no middle ground after his tirade. This was going to be a defining moment for this group, because obviously the head coach had just issued a challenge. Were we worthy of playing in the National Hockey League or were we just stealing paychecks like he suggested?

As the game started that night, the Edmonton Oilers never stood a chance. We came out like a group of caged gorillas who were hell-bent on causing destruction. Within the first minute of the game, there were four fighting majors handed out. Chris Clark—who had been mockingly referred to as a "warrior" by Darryl in the morning—dropped the gloves with Scott Ferguson. At the same time, Dave Lowry fought Ethan Moreau and from that point forward, it was like an old-school Battle of Alberta.

That night, Jarome Iginla and Shean Donovan also got into fights for our team, but Krzysztof Oliwa was the shining star. Just a few hours after Darryl lit into him and questioned why he was even playing in the NHL, Oliwa had a great fight with Oilers tough guy Georges Laraque. And then Oliwa did something even more unexpected: He scored a goal.

Oliwa scored a highlight-reel goal on Edmonton netminder Tommy Salo—for one of his 17 career goals in the NHL. The funny thing is that Krzysztof only played 4:13 that night, but he certainly made the most of it. And considering he took the brunt of Darryl's venom earlier in the day, it was probably one of the sweetest games he ever played in the NHL.

We won the game 4–2 over the Oilers, outshooting them and racking up 48 minutes in penalties in the process. Jarome Iginla was an absolute beast that night, picking up a goal and two assists in addition to his fight. Darryl's pre-game rant had worked and his handling of the team was a big factor in why this group advanced to the Stanley Cup final a few months later. To this day, everybody who was in that room for Darryl's speech remembers it like it happened yesterday. If I'm having lunch with Matthew Lombardi or catching up with Shean Donovan, we're able to quote direct lines from that Sutter speech. It's engrained in our heads as the most powerful, tough, yet hilarious pre-game speech we've ever experienced— provided it wasn't directed at you.

Now, as a head coach, you can't give that type of speech 82 nights of the year, or else your team would tune you out pretty quickly. So Darryl was very good at picking his spots and knowing exactly what buttons needed to be pushed. I used to love to watch the way he motivated players like Jarome Iginla and Miikka Kiprusoff, because coaches always have to be careful in their treatment of star players.

For example, if we were hosting the Carolina Hurricanes in our building for a meaningless game in the middle of November, Darryl would find a way to motivate Iggy.

"Hey, Jarome, did you know you haven't scored a home goal against the Hurricanes in eight years?"

And sure enough, Jarome would go out that night and score a goal.

Or if we had a game down in Phoenix, he would try to light a fire under Jarome in another way.

"Iggy, you're up against your buddy Shane Doan tonight. Are you going to be better than him? Because if you're not, we have no chance to win."

He would do the same thing to Kiprusoff, issuing him a challenge in front of everyone else. "Miikka, if you're not better than Cam Ward tonight, then we can't win this game. We need you."

It was a way to issue a challenge to the stars, but also make them feel important. He was very respectful toward Iginla and Kiprusoff because he knew they were the key to the team's success. Darryl was a master motivator behind the bench and we actually loved playing for him. Even after a speech like he gave us in Edmonton, we would still go through a wall for Darryl

Sutter because he believed in our group. He just had to find different ways to bring out the best in us.

Sometimes, he would even resort to physically trying to motivate his players behind the bench. Not too many people know this, but Darryl would occasionally give his players a little boot in the ass when he was pacing back and forth behind the bench. It wasn't like he gave them a big kick—but it was hard enough for the player to know that he was over their shoulder. I used to have a great vantage point for these little kicks since I was sitting at the end of the bench as the backup.

One time we were in Montreal and the Canadiens had jumped out to a quick 3–0 lead against us. Darryl was pacing up and down the bench when he stopped between Jarome Iginla and Craig Conroy. He gave Conroy a kick to the back and then leaned down to the two of them and said, "Are you guys going to take your fucking dresses off and hit somebody— or are you just going to float all night?"

Conroy was so fired up from this kick in the pants that he went out and accidentally took a five-minute major penalty for boarding on the very next shift. We ended up coming back to tie that game, so once again Darryl showed off the power of his unique motivational skills.

While he would kick guys in the backside when he was angry, Darryl was also known to be physical in a positive way. After every win, he would make sure he shook hands with every player in the dressing room. And his way of saying "I love you" was a playful punch in the shoulder or a little pull of your hair. It meant the world to us to get that approval from Darryl after a game. The guy just lived and breathed the game, so to make him happy meant you had played the right way.

A big reason we loved Darryl was that he was very protective of his players when it came to the media. It was okay for him to rip us behind closed doors, but if a media member tried to do the same on the air or in the newspaper, then Darryl went ballistic. To him, it was almost like he was the head of the family; it's okay for family members to say mean things about each other, but the minute an outsider tries to say something, everybody goes into full protect mode. I can spank my own children, but don't you dare raise a hand to them.

And that's what was amazing about Darryl: Not only did he get to know you as a player, but he did his research on your family life, what your upbringing was like, if you had any brothers or sisters and what your parents were like. He genuinely took an interest in family because he was truly a caring guy when it came to the whole package as a player. That is why he is a great coach and person—and the very same reason almost all his players, current and former, love him. They know he can be hard, but underneath his tough delivery and brash style they know he cares about them as people.

There were many times when he came to Jarome Iginla's defense in the media after some of the beat writers were critical of him. In the playoffs one year against Detroit, the writers were criticizing Iginla and Darryl went to the podium in front of all the television cameras and just went at the media. He accused the writers that day of not doing their homework and he basically poured cold water on their stories.

And while he had the reputation of being a hard-ass and a disciplinarian, he knew exactly when his players needed some space. If we lost a tough game on home ice on a Saturday night, he would walk into the dressing room post-game and say, "It's a day off tomorrow. I don't want to see you at the rink. Stay out of the medical room. Stay away from this rink. Now go fuck off and be with your families."

Darryl had a way of making even the term "fuck off" sound endearing and warm. But I suppose when you drop the F-bomb every two seconds, you're bound to find some positive uses for the word.

Jimmy Roberts and the Most Bizarre Post-game Speech

Some coaches I've had—such as Al Arbour, Mike Keenan and Darryl Sutter—are household names to most hockey fans in North America. But some of the most colorful stories I've witnessed from behind the bench were courtesy of a man named Jimmy Roberts.

The older generation of hockey fans would probably remember Roberts as a player. He played over a thousand games in the

NHL and won five Stanley Cups as a member of the Montreal Canadiens in the 1960s and 1970s. But Roberts also made his mark as a minor league hockey coach, winning a couple of championships with the Springfield Indians. He also coached a full season with the Hartford Whalers in 1991–92, but the stories about Jimmy Roberts's time in the minor leagues are legendary.

My first interaction with Roberts came when I was sent down to the Worcester Ice Cats of the American Hockey League. It was a shared affiliation between New York and St. Louis and the Islanders had demoted me to the AHL during the 1995–96 season. I had actually requested that Mike Milbury send me to Worcester and not Salt Lake City—the Islanders' other affiliate—because I knew the Blues organization might be interested in my services down the road. And if I could go to Worcester and impress their staff, I would have a good chance of signing there as a free agent in the summer.

I joined the Ice Cats in St. John's, Newfoundland, when they were in the middle of an east coast road trip. I didn't know many of the players since there were a lot of Blues prospects on the team, but I was happy to see Jason Strudwick in the visitors' dressing room when I arrived. We had both been drafted by the Islanders and had become instant friends two years earlier.

Also in the dressing room was an attendant who helped look after the visiting players' needs in St. John's. He would fill the Gatorade bottles, make sure we had towels and generally serve as an extra equipment guy for the road team. But this dressing room attendant had one striking physical trait that made him stand out: He was a little person. And I was about to find out that our coach, Jimmy Roberts, did not know the first thing about being politically correct.

About halfway through this game in St. John's, my buddy Jason Strudwick was having an awful night on the blue line. He turned the puck over and cost our team a couple of goals. From my perspective on the end of the bench, I could tell he was really fighting the puck. Roberts had the same vantage point as I did and he could also see Jason's struggles on the ice, so during a face-off in the neutral zone, Roberts yelled to Jason, "Just dump it in if you get it. Dump it in!"

Of course, we won the face-off and the puck came right onto Jason's stick. But he was mentally fragile at this point, having struggled for the whole game. So while Roberts was yelling, "Dump it in! Dump it in!" Jason promptly fanned on the shot. It was a big-time whiff from Jason that led directly to a turnover for the Maple Leafs. St. John's came down the ice and got another terrific scoring chance, but luckily we did not allow them to score. As the puck was frozen, Jason skated back to our bench with his head down in shame, knowing he was going to get an earful from Jimmy Roberts.

Jimmy laced into him.

"Hey, Strudwick, that fucking little bastard could shoot the puck harder than you!" he yelled, while pointing at our dressing room attendant.

I was sitting right next to the poor dressing room attendant and all I could think was that our head coach was certifi-
ably insane. This was my first game under Jimmy Roberts and
I couldn't believe what I'd just heard. I'm not sure who felt
worse—Jason for turning the puck over, or the dressing room
attendant for being used as a comic prop. Either way, I got my
first taste of Jimmy Roberts that night.

The next season, I saw the best side of Jimmy's legendary dry sense of humor. At this point, I was property of the
St. Louis Blues and we had just lost a game 8–1. It was one of
those nights when the whole team was terrible. I got the hook
after giving up four goals, but I'm sure it wasn't my fault—
ha-ha. Most of the guys were minus-four or minus-five and
not a single player had had a good night. We knew that Jimmy
would not be a happy man when he came in for his post-game
speech to the guys. It was one of those nights where a trash
can could get kicked over or a couple of sticks broken in anger.

Instead, Jimmy walked into the room holding a telephone
in his hand. He was in the middle of a conversation with
St. Louis general manager Mike Keenan.

"Oh no, Mike, it wasn't like that. Our guys played really
hard tonight. Don't let the 8–1 score fool you. They com-
peted," Jimmy said to our amazement.

At that point, we realized that the phone wasn't plugged
into the wall. He had an old-style phone, with the cord drag-
ging on the floor. Instead of ripping each of us to our face, he

decided to have a fake conversation with Mike Keenan, with the whole team as spectators. This was something straight out of a movie.

"McLennan? I would suggest you call him up right now. He's the best goalie in the American Hockey League. Don't worry about those four goals on six shots tonight. Those weren't his fault," he sneered.

And he basically called out every single player in this mock phone call, with the sarcasm just dripping from his voice.

"Jamie Rivers was a minus-four tonight, Mike, but don't let that scare you. I know he likes to hit guys, but he didn't hit anyone tonight. Don't worry about it—just call him up."

"You know what, Mike? I would suggest you send that whole St. Louis team down here and call all of these guys up. Because I guarantee you'll win up there with this crew."

When Jimmy walked out of the room that night, we all looked at each other and started to laugh. It was one of the funniest things we'd ever witnessed in a professional hockey dressing room.

In the end, Jimmy's message got through to us. We knew he was right and, as a player, you sometimes appreciate a message being delivered in unique way. A coach who yells and screams at you all the time will probably lose the room pretty quickly.

We came to expect that type of behavior from Jimmy because he was such a colorful character. He used to sit in his office with a bell on his desk. When he wanted an equipment guy to come in he would ring the bell once, and when he wanted a medical guy to come in he would ring it twice. We'd be sitting in the dressing room and we'd hear the bell ring. The equipment guys would leap up and start walking to his office—only to hear a second bell ring. It was one of those strange quirks that Jimmy had as a head coach.

He also preferred a non-verbal mode of communication when he was running practices on the ice. He never wore hockey gloves when he was on the ice; he wore regular winter gloves with hockey tape around the fingers. And then he would use a series of hand signals to dictate different drills. Instead of just yelling out, "Go faster!" he would simply twirl his hand in a circular motion and we knew it meant to speed up. He would weave his hands if he wanted us to do crossovers and so forth. He basically had hand signals for every drill you could imagine in a hockey practice.

But my most memorable practice with Jimmy Roberts had nothing to do with hand signals. When we were in Worcester, we used to put on all of our equipment at the game rink and then take a bus over to a practice facility. One day, I got to the practice facility in my full gear and realized that I had forgotten to pack my mask.

I phoned back to the main rink and luckily our trainer was still there. He said he would drive over to the practice facility with the mask in a few minutes, but I would have to be late getting onto the ice.

When Jimmy walked into the room, I explained the situation to him. "Jimmy, I'll be late for practice. I just have to wait for the guys to bring my mask over to this rink."

But Jimmy would have no part of it. "Get the fuck out on the ice," he barked at me. Reluctantly, I went onto the ice with no mask, like I was a goalie from the 1940s.

We were just skating around in warm-ups doing laps and I figured I'd be okay until my mask showed up. Suddenly, Jimmy blew his whistle and signaled for the start of shooting drills.

I once again pleaded my case with Jimmy, but to no avail. "Just get in the fucking net," he commanded me.

The guys started doing the long three-line drill, where they would basically take the puck the length of the ice and then shoot at the goalie. I took my position in the net with a huge lump in my throat, having only played road hockey without a mask. And getting hit in the face with a puck from a pro hockey player would probably feel a lot worse than taking a frozen tennis ball from one of your 11-year-old friends.

Fortunately, Jimmy also blew his whistle and said, "Hey, boys, keep the pucks down on this side. Only pucks below the knees on him," as he pointed in my direction. But I was still worried about a deflection or an errant puck catching me in the side of the head. As the guys were skating down the ice, they were laughing hysterically and taking these weak little wrist shots along the ice.

But one of my teammates—this apparent lunatic from Quebec named Marquis Mathieu—took a full slap shot that hit me at the top of my pads. Perhaps this kid didn't have the French translation for "keep the pucks down," but I was incensed that he would jeopardize my safety with a full slap shot.

Thankfully, the trainer showed up with my mask a few minutes later. As soon as I put it on, Jimmy skated by me and said, "It's like a soldier going to war without his helmet. Don't let it happen again."

Once again, it was a strange way to deliver a message, but it was a classic Jimmy Roberts story. And I have to admit, I never forgot my mask for another practice after that and I never forgot Jimmy. I had him a year later again as an assistant coach in St. Louis. He was a big part of my getting to the organization, as well as my getting back to the NHL after my Islanders days and my bout with meningitis. For that he will always have my respect as a great coach and even better man.

Keenan Gets Fired in St. Louis

There's a cliché in professional sports that says it's always easier to fire one coach than 20 players when things aren't going well.

While the coach is the one who often takes the fall, there is no worse feeling in a dressing room than watching somebody lose his job because of your poor performance.

It was really hard for us to watch Jim Playfair get let go from his coaching position in Calgary in June of 2007 because we had all really loved him as an assistant coach. In that earlier role, he had played good cop to Darryl Sutter's bad cop, and on some levels we still thought of him that way. When Jimmy made the move to head coach, it was a really difficult transition for him to make. We did make the playoffs and finish that season with 96 points under Jimmy, but the expectations were set so high in Calgary that it was almost impossible for anyone to succeed without going back to the Stanley Cup final. And when Jimmy was fired at the end of that season, it was really hard for us to handle. These head coaches have families—wives and children—and they have to live with the humiliation of being fired from a very high-profile position, not to mention the inconvenience and sadness of moving on.

For the most part, every coach tries to help you get better as an individual player. Each coach has his own set of tools for motivation, but the bottom line is they are just trying to get the most out of you. In Long Island I distinctly remember being upset to see Lorne Henning get fired.

He was our coach during the lockout-shortened 1994–95 season and it was the first season where I was pretty much exclusively on an NHL roster. Lorne tried so many different things to motivate us, but we finished in last place with just 35 points.

We all knew the writing was on the wall for Lorne, but we played our hearts out for him. I remember being moved almost to tears one day in the locker room because he tried to motivate us with the Garth Brooks song "Outside the Fire." I thought we just had to win for this guy because he cared so much. But Lorne was fired at the end of the season.

While Jimmy and Lorne lasted until the end of the year, the worst fate for a coach is to be replaced mid-season. That happened to Mike Keenan during my first season in St. Louis and it was quite the scene when it all went down.

I had just been called up to join the team from the farm club in the middle of December because Grant Fuhr was injured. I did the short drive from Worcester to Hartford, where the team was scheduled to play the Whalers. The Blues were coming off an 8–0 loss to the Vancouver Canucks in the previous game and, clearly, tensions were high inside the dressing room.

As we hit the ice for practice, you knew something was going to happen. In the very first drill, Keenan came down and fired a shot at my head. This was supposed to be a simple dump-in drill, but he decided to wire a slap shot right at me. He probably wouldn't have done that to Grant Fuhr, but maybe he figured he could make an example out of me. Fortunately, I got out of the way at the last second, but it certainly set the tone for a very bizarre practice.

The whole on-ice session that day in Hartford lasted about eight minutes. Mike skated the wind out of all of us; it was one of the most up-tempo, high-energy practices I had ever taken part in in my life. And even though the workout had lasted less than 10 minutes, I was covered in sweat and dead tired. Not many players were enamored with Mike's decision to make us work that hard on a game day.

Brett Hull, who was one of the greatest players to ever play this game, decided to speak his mind. Mike and Brett got into a heated exchange at center ice in front of the entire team. This was my first time up with the team all season, so it was my first window into the rumored rift between head coach and star player.

"You know what, Brett? It doesn't matter. You didn't like the guy before me. I'm here now and you hate me, and guess what? You're going to hate the guy after me too," Mike said to him very loudly. With those words, it almost sounded like Mike knew his fate with the Blues was sealed.

"Fuck you. You're brutal," said Hull, who was clearly tired of having Mike as a head coach.

The practice basically ended on that note; an eight-minute session highlighted by Mike shooting a puck at my head and then challenging Brett Hull in front of the rest of the team. That night, I watched from the bench as we lost a 5–3 game to the Hartford Whalers with Jon Casey in net.

We flew back to St. Louis and there was a sense that the other shoe was about to drop. We were scheduled for a 10 a.m. team meeting followed by a practice at the arena—but it just kept getting pushed back later and later. We knew something was going down, because it was very strange to not hold a practice at the regularly scheduled time.

A few minutes after 11:00 a.m., Al MacInnis walked into the room and announced that Mike had been fired. And just like that, the Keenan era was over in St. Louis. That firing didn't resonate much with me because I had barely played for Mike in St. Louis, but it was a real eye-opener into the internal politics of an NHL team.

I know coaches are hired to be fired, but every time it happens, it still sends shockwaves through a dressing room.

5

Life in the Blue Paint

Of all the possible positions you can play in professional sports, a goaltender in hockey has the reputation of being the quirkiest and most superstitious of the bunch. You never hear about a forward described as "flaky" or "different," because those terms are usually reserved for the guys in the blue paint.

And the reputation is totally justified when you consider that some of us are known to talk to our goalposts, while others are fanatical about routines. For me, I used to touch both goalposts after every whistle in the game. It was a superstition and a habit, but it also allowed me to make sure I knew where I was in my net at all times. And after touching both posts, I would also go for a little skate to the corner.

I did this to refocus and reset my mind as the play was set to resume. If I ever forgot to go for the little skate to the corner, I never said to myself, "Oh no—I'm going to let a goal in now." I was superstitious, but I never was so fanatical about my routines that I thought they had a direct impact on my performance.

Now the one thing you never want to do is mess with a starting goalie's game-day routine.

When I was in the NHL, I had a strange ritual that I did before the start of every game. I would line up my goalie pads right in front of my locker stall, so they would be standing up and leaning on each other back-to-back. Then I used to take a black marker or Sharpie and I would draw a little black dot on the carpet or plastic mat right in between my pads.

I used to use this little black dot as a focal point, so I would sit there and stare at it for a few minutes. The reason I did this was to get focused on trying to find the little black dot— which represented the puck. In my mind, if I could pick out that little black dot on the rug, it would simulate trying to find the puck during a game situation. There are a lot of times during the game when a goalie loses sight of the puck during a crazy goal-mouth scramble. All you see are sticks, legs and players' bodies, and it's difficult to locate that little black puck. Sitting at my stall and staring at the little black dot on the floor before a game was a little mental imagery trick that I always found useful.

Of course, some of my teammates knew about this pre-game ritual and one of them would be sure to come by and knock my pads over while I was in deep concentration. That stuff always irritated me because I felt like I needed to get into a zone if I was going to be the starter. And toward the end of my career—when my starts became less and less frequent—I needed to make sure I was mentally sharp before each game. Looking back at the whole superstition, it may seem a little strange to an outsider, but it's something that really helped me out. And I never appreciated when teammates would disrupt the routine.

I also did not enjoy when people messed around with my equipment—especially my mask. To a goaltender, a mask is the most personal and sacred piece of equipment. And I hated when people would come and touch my mask—or even try it on—because I was always worried about the germs. When somebody picks up a goalie mask, they inevitably reach for it by grabbing at the facemask portion of the cage. And I always hated that, because that's exactly what my nose and mouth would be pressed up against inside the mask. I never knew where these people's fingers had been, so it was almost like they were sticking their fingers down my mouth when they decided to handle my mask.

Now, Miikka Kiprusoff knew about my dislike for people touching my mask, so he tried to get people to grab it as often as possible. At the end of a lot of home games at the Saddledome, there would be little tours of the dressing room. If players had friends or family in town, they'd often bring them by the room to meet some of the guys and get a behind-the-scenes tour of the room.

And of course they would be fascinated with the goalie equipment because it looked totally different than the gear used by the 18 other skaters. But nobody would go near Kipper's equipment, because it was usually soaking wet from the sweat of the 60-minute game he'd just played. So Kipper would yell from behind the curtain to a tour group, "Hey, try on Jamie McLennan's mask, he won't mind at all!"

Sure enough, people would start putting on my mask because Kipper had told them it was all right to do so. They would be breathing through my mask, taking pictures with it and getting their grubby hands all over my most personal piece of equipment. And I would absolutely go ballistic when I came into the room and saw my mask being used as a tourist attraction.

I remember flipping out at Andrew Ference one time, because one of his good friends was wearing my mask after Miikka told him to try it on.

"Hey, tell your friends they can't be putting on my shit!" I shouted at him. Of course Andrew felt bad because Kipper had told his buddies it was okay to try on my gear. And Miikka could always be found laughing behind the curtain, because he knew he had just helped create a big scene.

I also had another piece of equipment that my teammates liked to use as a source of comedy. I never liked the feeling of having a bare ass when wearing my jock strap, so I used to wear a little pair of underwear that looked like a Speedo under my gear.

One day, I was sitting in my stall and somebody whistled at me to look over and suddenly, my little Speedo underwear appeared at the top of the doorway. And then a blow torch showed up right underneath it—and set it on fire. It was absolutely one of the funniest pranks that ever got played on me and I have Marc Bergevin to thank for that one.

Bergevin was a hilarious prankster inside the dressing room and he would always fool teammates into autographing the wrong thing. One time in Ottawa, I walked into the room and he told me, "Hey Noodles, I need you to sign this jersey. Make sure you make it big because they want to see it."

So without thinking, I took a Sharpie and signed my name in big letters on the side of the jersey. A couple of minutes later, Craig Conroy came into the room and flipped out at me, demanding to know why I ruined a Brett Hull All-Star game jersey with my signature. Bergevin was sitting in the corner and howling at the controversy he had caused.

I somehow find it funny that he is now the general manager of the Montreal Canadiens, since he was such a prankster in his playing days. But Marc is also one of the most well-connected and intelligent people in the hockey world and I'm sure he'll get the Habs back on track.

Losing My Mind—and My Blocker

For a goaltender, there is no greater feeling of disappointment than taking a scoreless game into overtime and then giving up a goal. You work your tail off for more than 60 minutes only to lose the game and a chance at a shutout.

During the 2002–03 season, I unfortunately experienced the losing side of one of these heartbreaking games. We were in New York to play the Rangers at Madison Square Garden on November 7, having just come off victories in New Jersey and Long Island. We had the rare opportunity to pull off a sweep of all three New York-area teams and I was the starting goalie in each game. An injury had sidelined Roman Turek, so Greg Gilbert had given me the chance to start a few games in a row. I was really in a groove with those two straight wins and I felt like I was really on my game at MSG.

We battled the Rangers hard for 60 minutes and the game remained scoreless. While neither team had scored a goal, there had been plenty of scoring chances on both sides. I had made 33 saves during regulation time, while my counterpart Dan Blackburn had turned away 26 shots. This was clearly a goaltender's duel. And because this was the era before the shootout, there was a chance that we could finish with a 0–0 tie.

But less than one minute into overtime, the Rangers broke into our zone on a two-on-one. And this wasn't your average two-on-one either; this was Mark Messier with Brian Leetch. A couple of Hall of Famers were bearing down on me with the game on the line.

Messier had the puck and made the perfect play by forcing me to commit to the shot. He was able to fool me and send a seamless pass over to Leetch, who easily skated past me and put the puck into the empty net for the winning goal. Leetch had gotten away from Jarome Iginla, who was supposed to be covering him on the play. Luckily for Iggy, I don't hold grudges about these types of things.

The arena erupted when the red light went on and the Rangers' goal-scoring theme song overtook the loudspeaker. I was so upset that I took my goal stick and snapped it into two pieces over my knee.

As the Zamboni doors opened to allow us to leave, I was still really fired up. In frustration, I took one of the pieces of my broken goal stick and hurled it against the end boards. But when I threw the half-stick against the boards, my blocker went along with it for the ride. And naturally, my blocker sailed over the glass and into the netting behind our own goal.

So now my blocker was hanging there and I wasn't sure what to do. The Rangers crowd could be the most hostile crowd in the league, and I didn't want to risk the embarrassment of having to retrieve my blocker. I had played for the Islanders before, so they definitely knew who I was inside MSG. They would have really given it to me, with taunting and swearing (in that thick New York accent): "Hey, McLennan—you lost the game and your block-ah. You piece of shit!"

I wasn't really interested in hearing that at the moment.

Not only that, I wasn't sure how I was going to physically get the blocker down from the netting. This would be a two-person job and I didn't feel like having 18,500 fans witness my humiliation. Honestly, at that point, I would have been happy if a New York fan had just taken my blocker home as a souvenir. I was ready to tell the training staff to order me a new one because there was no way I was taking the time to try and get it back.

So, with the rare combination of anger and embarrassment surging through my veins, I simply skated off the ice and left my blocker hanging in the netting. I went into the visiting locker room at MSG and hopped into the shower. While I was in there, Scott Nichol walked in, with that shit-eating grin of his, and said, "Hey, I got your blocker back for you."

This came as a complete surprise to me, because I had already written off the blocker. Scotty had seen what had happened after the game and, being the good teammate that he was, he retrieved it for me. But it should be noted that, being the prankster that he was, Scotty also seized this as an opportunity to have ammunition to abuse me with down the road. He took his stick and basically fished out my blocker by himself. He added, "Don't worry, I don't think anybody else saw you do that."

I was really relieved to hear that double dose of good news. Not only had Scotty retrieved my blocker, but he was pretty sure that nobody had seen the entire episode unfold—except for him. I was starting to feel better about the incident until my brother Dave phoned me later that night.

"Hey, Jamie, you made the highlight reel tonight," he told me over the phone. "The sports show had you as the Alka-Seltzer upset play of the night. They had you tossing your stick and blocker after the overtime winner." They used to have a regular TV segment in which a person who was angry or embarrassed made the highlights in a segment sponsored by Alka-Seltzer. On that night, I was the winner of the dubious award, since the TV cameras had captured my blocker toss.

And now that it was out in the open, Scotty Nichol made sure he reminded me about his heroics. For the next two weeks, every time I was in the dressing room, Scotty would come up to me with my blocker attached to the end of his stick.

"Hey, Noodles, don't worry," he'd say. "I've got your blocker for you today."

Eating on the End of the Bench

Everybody who knows me is well aware of my passion for popcorn. I'm one of the only people who actually owns a movie theatre popcorn maker, because the microwavable bags just don't do it for me.

When I was at the rink, you could always find me munching on a little bit of popcorn. My habit really started in St. Louis, where our trainers would always have a couple of bags of popcorn lying around. I would grab a bag and walk around the room chatting with the guys. One of my roles as backup goalie was to make sure the guys were loose and ready before a game, and I figured if I could chat them up—while eating a bag of popcorn—they'd be very relaxed because I would give off a very casual demeanor. I would often ask them about the opposing goalie, where they'd like to shoot against him, so that they would start thinking about the game in a really positive manner.

While popcorn was a big part of my pre-game routine, I can't deny that I would also sometimes bring food onto the bench with me. When you're sitting at the end of the bench as a backup goalie, you tend to get hungry during the course of a hockey game. Of course, I had to be very discreet about eating on the bench because most head coaches didn't want to see their backup goalie with a mouthful of popcorn at a key moment during the game.

I developed a system where I would sneak food onto the bench and eat it without anybody noticing. There was a perfect spot at the top of my pads where I could secretly slide my food. I used to love little sweet snacks—like Gummi Bears and Jujubes—so I could put a few of them into my pads and it was like a little serving dish for me. I would place a towel over my knee, so that when I was sitting down, the coaching staff couldn't see my secret stash. Teammates used to use that towel to wipe their visors and sticks, so it actually served a dual purpose. And every so often, I would discreetly reach under the towel and grab a couple of Gummi bears and put them into my mouth.

Of course, my secret system wasn't exactly foolproof.

I was playing with the Florida Panthers and Roberto Luongo was having a tough night. Lou got the hook and I was summoned into the game from my spot on the bench. I was in such a rush to get into the game that I must have forgotten that the towel—which was, as usual, hiding my snack supply—was still on top of my knee.

I got into the game and made a couple of saves in the first minute or so. In the process of making those saves, the towel must have come out from inside my pad—and though I hadn't noticed, one of our defensemen had. Sean Hill grabbed the towel with his stick while the play was still going on.

One of the referees yelled at him, "Hey, what is that on your stick?"

Sean replied, "These fans are throwing towels on the ice. Blow the whistle!" But Sean knew exactly where that towel had come from, because he was one of the guys who would often wipe his visor using my towel.

We had a good chuckle about that after the game; Sean had a great sense of humor and he didn't mind covering up for my towel mishap on the ice. Fortunately for me, I didn't have a dozen Gummi Bears come spilling out of my pads that night as well.

There was a time, though, when I was caught in a food-related incident at the Bell Centre in Montreal. For those of you who have had the pleasure of going to a Canadiens game—either at the old Forum or the new rink—you know how special the hot dogs are inside that arena. It's really hard to describe, because if you ate that hot dog anywhere else in the world, it would be gross. It's basically a boiled wiener served on a piece of lightly toasted Wonder bread. But for some reason, it's the most special and delicious hot dog when you're inside the Bell Centre.

And when you're at the rink in Montreal, these hot dogs are everywhere. The concession stands are full of them, the press room has them at all times and of course, they filter their way down to the locker rooms. The trainers and dressing room attendants are always running around with a couple of hot dogs and delivering them to somebody.

I was backing up one night at the Bell Centre when I was playing with the Blues and I definitely had a hankering for one of those hot dogs. The strange thing about the Bell Centre is that the backup goalie doesn't actually sit at the end of the bench with his teammates. Somehow, they didn't have the foresight—in 1996—to make the benches long enough so that the backup could sit with his teammates. It's the most ridiculous design concept you can ever imagine: the backup goaltender has to sit by himself, directly across the ice surface from the players' benches, near the tunnel where the players come on and off the ice. Being isolated like that, you don't have any contact with your teammates.

So you really felt like an idiot, dressed in all your goalie gear—but not sitting with your teammates. It was like being a paid spectator at the game, surrounded by fans. And when you were sitting that close to the fans, you inevitably got a whiff and a view of those hot dogs. And, soon enough, you had a craving for one of them.

On this night, one of the dressing room attendants happened to have a couple of extra hot dogs. He gave me one at the start of the period and I discreetly slipped it into my glove. Even though I was across the ice from my teammates, I didn't want anybody to see me eating the hot dog during the game. Every minute or so, I would pretend to scratch my face with my glove—but I was secretly taking a bite of the hot dog. And this was in the era before cell phone cameras and Twitter, so there was no danger of a fan really catching me and announcing to the world that I had eaten a hot dog during a game.

I was able to eat the hot dog without anybody noticing—or so I thought. After the period ended, the team came back into the locker room for the intermission. One of the trainers told me that Joel Quenneville wanted to see me inside his office. I thought it was strange that the coach would want to talk to me in the middle of a game, considering I couldn't really offer up any insight from my vantage point. But maybe he wanted to ask me about how Grant was playing or if I had any tips on Jeff Hackett in the Montreal goal.

I walked into the office, fully expecting Joel to ask me a question about the game.

"So, did you like that hot dog?" he asked me directly.

I was caught completely off-guard. How in the world had Joel seen me eating a hot dog from 100 feet away while a game was going on? I pretended to play dumb, because I thought he must have been joking.

"Ummm...what are you talking about?" I replied.

"Did you like the hot dog you were eating during the second period?" he asked again.

I had been caught red-handed. Somehow, Joel had seen through my hidden hot-dog-in-the-glove trick to realize I had eaten one during the second period. I had no choice but to confess.

"Well, they are pretty good, right?" I said with a sheepish smile.

Joel looked right at me and started to smile. Then he motioned his hand toward a table and there was a stack of hot dogs sitting there. It turns out the coaches enjoyed the hot dogs so much that they were eating them between periods.

"So, do you want another one?" he asked me.

"No thanks, I'm good," I replied. "I've already had a couple tonight."

And with that, I walked out of the room, feeling really embarrassed. I still have no idea how Joel and the coaching staff saw me eating the hot dog that night. But the amazing thing about Joel is that he never made an issue out of the incident after that. If there was ever a coach who was going to bust you for trying to sneak a hot dog during a game, you wanted it to be Joel Quenneville.

If I couldn't sneak a hot dog past the coach when I was 100 feet away from him, just imagine how difficult it was to try and eat food when I was sitting right there on the end of the bench. In Toronto, the backup goaltender sits at the far end of the bench, right next to the paying customers. One night when I was there with the Flames, I was sitting on the end of the bench next to a couple who were on a date.

I would often engage in a little conversation with the fans during the game, because it's hard not to speak to someone who is two feet away from you for the whole night. I was always a laid-back and friendly guy, so if a fan wanted to speak to me a little bit, I would definitely respond. On this night, the guy was chatting with me and asking some questions at different points during the game.

"Hey, do you want me to get you some food?" he asked. The couple had been eating all night long, with a steady stream of hot dogs, pretzels and nachos coming to their seats.

"Sure. Why don't you get me some nachos?" I replied.

"Are you serious?"

"Yeah, why not? Those nachos you guys were eating earlier looked pretty good to me. You can't get me a whole order of nachos because that will look bad. But I'll share some with you if you guys don't mind my hands."

I think he was totally stunned. He was asking me as a joke if I wanted any food and now I was actually putting in an order for nachos at the Air Canada Centre. At that point in the game, I knew Miikka was having a good night, so there was no chance I was going to get thrown into action. If I shared a little nacho platter with some fans, it wouldn't be the worst thing in the world.

Of course, I didn't want Darryl Sutter to see me eating nachos at the end of the bench, because I'm pretty sure he wouldn't have been as forgiving as Joel Quenneville with the hot dog. So this couple placed the nachos down by their feet and every so often, I would reach down like I was pretending to grab my water bottle. But I was really grabbing a nacho and making sure that nobody else would see me.

So the next time you see a backup goalie on the end of the bench, you might want to keep your eye on him. Sometimes he can be just as entertaining as the game—when he's hungry.

The Best Saves—and Worst Goals—of My Career

When you say the names of goaltenders like Dan Cloutier and Tommy Salo, only one thing comes to mind: Bad goals.

Giving up weak goals is an occupational hazard of a professional goalie.

During the course of my career, I gave up a number of bad, soft and fluky goals. A few of them stand out in my mind.

During the 1994–95 season, I had the chance to start a game against the Bruins in the old Boston Garden. I was feeling great at the start of this game, as I distinctly remember robbing Ray Bourque in the first period. I made a skate save on Bourque's initial shot and then with the net wide open, I took away his rebound chance with a desperation save with my goal stick.

I was a young goalie at this point—only 23 years old—so I definitely remember being blown away by the fact I had just robbed a future Hall of Famer in Ray Bourque. That gave me a lot of confidence and our team was playing great that night. With goals from Pat Flatley, Benoit Hogue and Pierre Turgeon, we had jumped out to a 3–1 lead on the Bruins.

This was definitely going to be a night for me to remember. Except that it turned out to be a memorable game for all the wrong reasons.

Late in the second period, Cam Neely scored against me to cut our lead to 3–2 heading into the intermission. I still felt like we were in control of the game with 20 minutes left to play. But then, early in the third period, Bourque figured out a way to beat me—and suddenly the game was tied 3–3. All of those good feelings from the first period had evaporated and I was starting to feel the momentum swing in the Bruins' favor.

A couple of minutes after Boston tied the game, Neely took a slap shot toward the net from our blue line. There was nobody in front of me providing a screen, yet the puck beat me clean through the five-hole. Talk about a deflating moment; we had squandered a 3–1 lead on the road in Boston and the backbreaker was a terrible goal that I allowed from 60 feet away.

I could try and rationalize the goal by saying, "Hey, this is Cam Neely we're talking about in the Boston Garden. This rink is smaller than any other in the league, so a Neely slapper from the blue line really isn't that bad." But in reality the goal was a stinker, no matter how I tried to sugarcoat it. If I'd been screened or the puck had been tipped that would have been one thing. But Neely had beaten me with a relatively harmless slapper right through the five-hole.

I suppose if you're going to give up some soft goals, you may as well give them up to Hall of Famers. Another time, I had a horrible goal scored against me by Steve Yzerman during a playoff series against Detroit.

It was the final game of the 1998 playoff series between the Blues and Red Wings and Detroit had stormed out to a 5–1 lead. The series was all but over and Joel Quenneville thought the only humane thing to do was to pull Grant Fuhr out of the nets.

Detroit was basically just trying to run out the clock and make sure none of their star players got hurt for the next series. They were the defending Stanley Cup champions (and as luck would have it, they would go on to repeat that result in 1998 as well).

Late in the game, Yzerman had the puck in the corner behind the goal line. He was surveying his options in front of the net and I made the mistake of looking to see where he might pass the puck. I must have come off my post by an inch or two and when that happened, Yzerman fired the puck toward the net. As luck would have it—although it wasn't luck on his part; it was a skill play—the puck ricocheted off the back of my knee and into the net.

The funniest thing about the whole situation is that Yzerman looked like he felt terrible about scoring that goal. The look on his face was a mixture of embarrassment and disbelief.

He actually mouthed an apology to me as his teammates came over to sheepishly celebrate.

I could read his lips as he said, "Sorry, Jamie."

On one hand it was funny that Steve Yzerman knew my name. On the other, I felt very humiliated that he exposed my mistake in the net that resulted in a goal for his team. With a player like Yzerman, a goaltender should always be prepared for something like that to happen because he was such an intelligent player.

At other times, an advance scouting report didn't actually help when it came to trying to stop a superstar sniper.

We were playing the Penguins one night during the 1994–95 season when Jaromir Jagr was in his prime in Pittsburgh. He ended up winning the first of his five Art Ross Trophies that season as the league's scoring leader and he already had the reputation as one of the most skilled and lethal forwards in the NHL.

In the dressing room prior to the game, my Islanders teammate Troy Loney came over to me with some advice about Jagr. Loney had played on the Penguins' two Stanley Cup teams with Jagr, so I was eager to get his advance scouting report on the superstar.

"If Jagr gets a breakaway on you, just remember that he always goes backhand," Loney told me.

That was a very helpful piece of advice coming from a former Penguins teammate.

Well sure enough, partway through the game, the Penguins sprang Jagr for a clean breakaway. As he moved into our zone, Loney's advice echoed in my head: "Remember, he always goes backhand."

I figured my best move would be to poke-check him because as he brought the puck to his backhand, he would likely have his head down. As he came in, I lunged out to poke-check him—but I must have been way too aggressive.

Jagr read my move and instead of going to his patented backhand move, he deftly skated around me and put the puck into the empty net on his forehand. So much for that pre-game scouting report.

After the game, while I was sitting in my stall, Loney came up to me and sort of apologized for the faulty intel.

"Well, I've never seen him make that move before. I guess he's added some new stuff to his arsenal."

All I could do was laugh, because Jagr had made me look pretty foolish.

There are other situations when you don't have as much time to prepare as a player comes in on a breakaway against you. The one player who gave me no time to create a strategy was Pavel Bure, who was absolutely the fastest opponent I ever played against.

When he was with the Canucks, Bure came in on a breakaway against me. I swear it was like he went from the red line to our face-off circle in less than a second, because all of a sudden he was right on top of me.

I didn't have any time to react and he fired a slap shot that rung off the post and into the net. I literally didn't have time to get set or prepare myself. The whole thing unfolded in a matter of three or four seconds. In situations like that, no amount of advance scouting—whether it was accurate or not—would have helped.

Even though Bure got the best of me that night, I did exact a measure of revenge against him a couple of years later. I was able to stop him on three breakaways while posting a shutout against the Canucks in Vancouver.

But for all the bad goals and moments that you remember during the course of your career, the great saves and memories will always outweigh them.

Probably the best save I ever made came during a game against the Philadelphia Flyers. I was in my second season in the league, playing with the Islanders, and we had jumped out to a 4–0 lead against the Flyers. It was the first time I went head-to-head against Ron Hextall, so I was pretty excited about the opportunity to beat my old mentor. But Philadelphia started chipping away at the lead with a couple of goals from Eric Lindros and then, all of a sudden, it was a 4–3 game in the dying minutes.

Rod Brind'Amour had a great chance to tie the game, as he was alone in the slot to my left. Brent Fedyk passed him the puck on a two-on-one and Brind'Amour had a wide open net to tie the game. In a desperation move, I reached over to my left and flung my glove out in an attempt to stop him. Brind'Amour shot the puck into my outstretched glove and it was probably the most spectacular save I have ever made in my life.

Darius Kasparaitis, our defenseman, was so impressed he came by and hugged me after the save, because he knew I had just saved everybody's bacon. We ended up holding on for a 4–3 win and that last-minute save against Brind'Amour stands out as one of my favorites.

I also made another memorable glove-hand save off Dale Hawerchuk one night when we were playing against the Buffalo Sabres. It was a neutral-site game between the Islanders and Sabres that was being played in Saint Paul, Minnesota. I was going head-to-head against Dominik Hasek, who was just starting to assert himself as the best goalie on the planet.

I was locked in a goalie's duel with Hasek and with the game tied in the third period, I robbed Hawerchuk of a sure-fire goal. He took a pass from behind the net and fired a one-timer that was destined to go in behind me. Fortunately for me, he shot the puck right into my glove—and I really sold it as a spectacular save.

I went on to match Hasek, save-for-save, the rest of that night, and we skated to a 2–2 tie. Both Hasek and I were named game stars, as I made 33 saves and he made 32 during the game. A couple of years later, I even beat Hasek in another head-to-head game.

Even though I certainly remember some soft goals during the course of my career, I like to remember the great moments too, like going toe-to-toe with Hasek.

Trying to Play Through an Injury

For most players in the NHL, playing through an injury is just a normal part of everyday life. Over the course of a grueling 82-game schedule, you end up with injuries that limit your ability to perform to the highest level on a nightly basis. You end up playing through injuries—both minor and serious—because you don't want the reputation of being a player who is constantly hurt. Once fans think you are someone who isn't willing to play through pain, it's very hard to shake that label.

But for goalies, playing through pain is a more difficult challenge than it is for positional players. A second-line winger can nurse a shoulder injury by making sure he doesn't throw any devastating body checks. A defenseman with a sore hand will make sure he doesn't wind up to take a slap shot from the point; he'll look to pass to his teammates instead.

Goaltenders, on the other hand, have no real way of hiding an injury. We can't say to ourselves, "Well, tonight I just won't make any saves with my left pad because that knee is hurting." We are the last line of defense and we have to be able to make the save. The position is so reactionary; we have no option of trying to protect injuries. When you're trying to stop a 100-mph slap shot from Al MacInnis, you don't have the luxury of choosing which part of the body you use to stop it. You make the save on instinct and deal with the fallout later.

I always tried to play through injuries in the crease. I never wanted to come out and jeopardize my career, because a big part of my job description as backup goaltender was to always be available. I didn't want the coach finding out that I had something nagging me because he needed to have full confidence to use me whenever he saw fit. A backup goalie who is often nursing an injury will find himself out of an NHL job in a hurry. Reliability is almost as important as performance on the ice.

When I was with the St. Louis Blues, I suffered a pretty bad injury to my right hand during a morning skate. It turns out I had not only fractured my thumb, but I had ruptured the sac that holds the thumb and index finger together. The whole area was swollen to about three times the size of my normal hand, but I didn't want to complain. I could barely hold my goal stick in my hand, but there was no way I was letting Rich Parent—our minor league goalie—come in and take my spot. I had battled back from meningitis, so I wasn't going to let a broken thumb get in the way of my NHL career. I had the training staff put a soft cast on my hand and I figured I'd be fine to serve as the backup goaltender. After all, Grant Fuhr was going to get the bulk of playing time in the nets anyway. I just needed to make sure I was able to practice with the guys and would only see game action if there was an emergency.

Well, sure enough, we were in San Jose on February 26, 1998, and Grant blew out his knee early in the hockey game.

I was thrust into action with a broken thumb, so I had to have one of the trainers—gritty Ray Barile—cut off my cast. During every TV timeout of that game, I would have him spray a numbing agent on my hand so that I could try and hold my stick without any pain. I finished off that game and ended up having to carry the ball for the next couple of weeks.

The remarkable thing is that we started a six-game winning streak the next night in Los Angeles and I was in goal for every game with my injured hand. I even posted shutouts over the Montreal Canadiens and Vancouver Canucks in the process. It was one of the most satisfying—yet challenging—stretches of my career. It's amazing what some adrenaline will do for you to help compensate for an injury. What would have happened if Rich Parent had been allowed to play those games? I'm glad I never found out.

In the 2003–04 season with the Calgary Flames I suffered what was probably the worst injury of my career. And as you might expect, I once again tried everything I could to play through the pain.

We were playing the Boston Bruins on December 18 and I was starting that night to give Miikka Kiprusoff a night off. Early in the first period, Bruins winger Brian Rolston came down the wing and let go of a cannon of a shot. I barely had time to react, because Rolston had one of the hardest shots in the league. As the puck came toward my upper chest, I made sure I was in position to make the save. But in doing so, my chest protector had shifted slightly, so when the puck hit me, it hit me square in my collarbone and sternum area—which had been left unprotected.

The force of the shot—which came from about 20 feet away—momentarily knocked the wind out of me. But as the play resumed at the other end of the ice, I could feel there was also a significant lump at the top of my chest. This puck had caught me square on my exposed skin; there was just no padding where it had hit me.

At the first TV timeout, I skated over to the bench and told the trainers what had happened. I told them I was just fine—which was true, because at that point the adrenaline had taken over and was completely masking the pain. When you're a backup goalie getting a chance to start a game in Boston, you don't come out because of a bump on your chest. Besides, I was feeling pretty good and hadn't allowed a goal through the first few minutes of the game. I think Rolston's shot was only the second one the Bruins had fired on me in the game, so I felt pretty fresh.

My focused play continued throughout the game and, with the help of my teammates, I recorded a shutout that night in Boston. I made 30 saves in a 5–0 win, with 28 of those stops coming after I suffered the injury. At various times I felt some numbness and tingling in my arms, but I was able to ignore the pain and weird feeling over the course of 60 minutes. Recording a rare shutout is always satisfying, but notching one when you're battling through something is probably the best feeling for a goaltender.

However, when the game ended and my adrenaline rush had subsided, I realized that I was in significant pain. I told our training staff about my situation and they immediately set up an X-ray of my collarbone. We went into the Bruins' medical area inside the rink and had their doctors take an X-ray to see if they could diagnose the damage. But I had some blood that had pooled up in the area, so the X-ray results came back inconclusive. At this point, we were still hopeful that it was just a severely bruised chest muscle.

I was in a ton of pain that night as we flew to Columbus, since we had a game against the Blue Jackets the very next night. I could barely sleep at the hotel that night, as I had trouble breathing and had to lie on my back. I knew I had to go to the rink in the morning for the optional skate, because the backup goalie always had to be available to take some shots.

But when I got to the rink that morning, I couldn't even lift up my arms. Something was terribly wrong inside my chest and the pain was radiating out to my extremities. The training staff instructed me not to go onto the ice in case I made the situation worse. They told me they would like to do further tests on me when we got back to Calgary the next day, but for that night in Columbus, I was basically going to be a spectator. Miikka was starting the game, so I didn't have to worry about seeing any game action against the Blue Jackets. During the warm-up that night, the guys were even careful not to shoot any pucks in my direction.

Miikka played that night in Columbus and in his typical fashion, he was stellar in a 2–1 victory and didn't need any help from me. When we got back to Calgary, I was still in a tremendous amount of pain. I phoned our trainer and I distinctly remember saying, "Something just doesn't feel right here. I can't move my arms and I get some tingling sometimes."

Our staff referred me for a CT scan at a medical clinic in Calgary, which would give them a much better picture than the X-ray did a couple of days earlier in Boston. I went in for the scan and within a couple of hours, our trainer phoned me back to tell me there were some serious issues.

"You've got a chipped clavicle and a fractured sternum," he told me over the phone. "This is very serious because the sternum is fractured in a couple of places. If you stop a puck there, it could stop your heart."

My immediate reaction was to figure out what I could do to solve the problem without going on injured reserve. We had a couple of young goalies in the minors who were eager to make their mark in the National Hockey League. Just like I made sure Rich Parent didn't get an opportunity in St. Louis, the last thing I wanted to do was give one of the Flames farmhands an opening to make an impression on the front office.

I had sought out the expertise of a chest specialist in Calgary, but he wasn't much help to me. Most of the serious sternum injuries he had treated were the result of car accidents, when the steering wheel was driven through someone's chest. There was basically no precedent of a goalie having a sternum injury as a result of stopping a puck.

I told our head coach and general manager Darryl Sutter that I wanted to do everything possible to play through this injury. I remember walking into his office at the Saddledome and telling him bluntly, "Look, I'll sign a waiver or whatever. I just want to keep playing."

So, after a conversation with Darryl and our medical staff, they agreed to let me play through the injury. We all figured that Miikka was going to be starting the bulk of the games for the next two weeks anyway, so I would have ample time to heal up. There was no sense in putting me on injured reserve and paying the salary of another goalie who was just going to sit at the end of the bench and watch Miikka start each game. Roman Turek was already sidelined with a knee injury, so they figured it was easier just to use me than to rely on an unproven kid from the minors.

While I wasn't going to see any game action, I did have to fulfill my role of backup goaltender in practice. That meant I was often the first goalie on and the last one off and it was an extremely painful experience. I could barely move my arms, so I was essentially a cardboard cutout who had lateral movement in the crease. And each time I did try to move my arms, I could feel a creaking and even hear a cracking sound coming from the middle of my chest.

I was able to manage the pain during these practices and figured I was well on my way to recovery when the worst possible thing happened: Kipper got hurt. We were playing the Minnesota Wild and Miikka tweaked his knee during a game that finished in a 2–2 tie. The initial diagnosis was that he was going to be sidelined for about two or three weeks, which meant I was suddenly thrust into the starting role with a fractured sternum. I was having a hard enough time getting through practices and now I was being counted on to win some important games for our team.

The next stretch was the toughest of my career, as I started eight consecutive games while in excruciating pain. I lost my first game on New Year's Eve, dropping a tough 2–1 decision to the Colorado Avalanche. But I turned things around the following week, when we went on an east coast road trip. I was able to post a shutout at Madison Square Garden as we beat the Rangers 5–0. And then, the very next night, we went to Long Island and I beat my old team in a hard-fought 3–2 game. In a span of 24 hours, I stopped 67 of 69 shots faced and picked up back-to-back victories over the two New York teams.

I was starting to feel pretty good about my game, despite the crippling injury. A couple of days after those wins in New York, I outdueled my old buddy Roberto Luongo as we beat the

Florida Panthers 4–2 at the Saddledome. But that was the last high point for me during this unforgettable stretch of games.

On January 14, we played a game in Washington at the Verizon Center. I was locked in a great duel with Olaf Kolzig and the game was scoreless going into the third period. But then the floodgates opened for both teams. Jarome Iginla scored for us; then Trent Whitfield replied for them. Moments later, Oleg Saprykin restored the lead for us. We were up 2–1 with just a few minutes to play in the game.

Sergei Gonchar had the puck at our blue line and he wound up for a slap shot that I could see coming. I was able to make a glove save on the puck initially, but then I was overcome with tremendous pain. Because I had to sort of reach back with my arm to make the glove save, it basically tore my chest apart. And since I was in so much pain, I ended up having to let go of the puck and it trickled into the net behind me. It all happened so fast, but I knew the injury had finally caught up to me. I had felt something tear inside my chest and I knew that I had made the injury worse.

But I stayed in the game and—miraculously—we took the lead 3–2 on a goal from Matthew Lombardi. We were just 30 seconds away from winning this game and from me escaping the Verizon Center with two points and a torn chest muscle. Of course, that's not the way the script went for me.

In the dying seconds of the game, I gave up what was likely the worst goal of my career, a goal that allowed the Capitals to tie the score. Jaromir Jagr had the puck in the corner behind the net and he fired a desperation shot toward me as the score clock counted down to zero. The puck rolled up the side of the net, glanced off the post and somehow, bounced off the inside of my knee and into the net as time expired. Jagr has scored a lot of highlight-reel goals in his NHL career, but this is one that wouldn't make it onto his greatest plays DVD. It was an awful goal to give up at any point in a hockey game, let alone in the dying seconds of a one-goal contest.

The game went into overtime and neither team scored, so it actually ended as a 3–3 tie. But I knew I had cost my team a point, so I went to Darryl after the game and told him that I was too injured to play. "I think now I'm just hurting the team," I admitted to him.

The next morning, he put me on the injured reserve list and Roman Turek was ready to come back and play for the next few games until Miikka was healthy again. I ended up on the shelf for a couple of weeks. Shortly thereafter, I was traded to the New York Rangers. Maybe Glen Sather was impressed with the fact that I had shut them out a few weeks earlier with my injury at MSG. I was really sad to get traded from the Flames, because that group was such a tightly knit team inside the dressing room.

I knew we were in for something special and although it was extremely difficult to watch them march all the way to the Stanley Cup final without me that spring, I was happy for them. When you love a team and an organization, you feel like you would go through a brick wall for them. That's how I felt about the Flames that year. I look back and I wouldn't change a thing—it was worth fighting through some pain for that experience.

My Near-Death Experience

While you can play through a lot of injuries in the NHL, sometimes there are circumstances that become more serious than a standard dislocated shoulder or torn muscle. And in the summer of 1996, I found out just how fragile life can really be.

When you are a 25-year-old athlete in the prime of your career, illness and death never cross your mind. We are well-conditioned athletes who are closely monitored by some of the best medical staffs on a daily basis. There is almost a feeling of being invincible.

During the 1995–96 hockey season, I bounced around quite a bit. I played a handful of games in the NHL with the New York Islanders, but I also spent a significant amount of time in the minors. We had affiliates in Worcester and Salt Lake City and I shuttled between those cities during that winter.

At the end of the season, I was tying up some loose ends— which is pretty difficult when you've spent time in three different cities in the past few months. There are cars, apartments and other logistical things that have to be dealt with before the start of summer. I decided that I would head from New York to Salt Lake City and then drive from there up to Alberta.

En route to my home in Alberta, I stopped in Lethbridge, where I had made a lot of close friends during my time in juniors. The Dyck family—my old billets from my days with the Hurricanes—still lived in town and I always relished the chance to go back and meet up with them. Their sons, Joel and Mike, are still two of my closest friends and we were going to catch up with each other.

I arrived at the Dyck house around 6 p.m. after the long drive from Salt Lake City. I wasn't feeling all that great, but I chalked it up to the fact that I had been traveling a lot in the past few days. With all those details to take care of, I had ended up flying from Worcester to New York to Salt Lake City and then driving up to Lethbridge—all in the span of about seven days.

We were out having a beer and shooting some pool when I started getting some severe cramps in my arms. I told Joel and Mike that it would be best if we returned to their house because I wasn't feeling all that great.

Earlier in the night, Joel had cooked us chicken for dinner and I started thinking that it wasn't sitting right. I kept accusing Joel of giving me food poisoning, but nobody else seemed to be having any problems digesting the chicken.

I started vomiting shortly after we returned to their home and realized that I was running a high fever as well. They decided to take me to the hospital around 11 p.m. because I just couldn't stop vomiting. But when we got to the hospital, they quickly sent us back home. They told us there was a nasty flu bug going around and my best plan of action was to just go back home and sleep it off.

So we went back to the Dyck house, but I could not sleep it off. I kept waking up every 30 minutes or so and vomiting. By the early morning hours, I had nothing left in my system. I was just throwing up green bile and stomach acid. I had completely lost my strength and I was starting to get very worried.

Joel and Mike's parents were both schoolteachers, so they were awake around 6:30 a.m. I called out to their mom and told her that something just wasn't quite right. She said that we should give it one hour and if the vomiting and fever didn't improve, we should go back to the hospital.

So around 7:30 a.m. Joel and Mike took me back to the same hospital to get medical attention. Shortly after we arrived, another patient came in with cardiac arrest, so they obviously gave that person priority over me. While I was waiting for them to admit me, I was lying on the bathroom floor and throwing up.

Finally, they got me into emergency and immediately hooked me up to an IV. I had been completely dehydrated by vomiting nonstop for the past 12 hours. I figured once I had some fluids in me, they would discharge me and diagnose this as a case of severe food poisoning.

But the doctor started asking me some bizarre questions that really set off my alarm bells.

"Are you an IV drug user?" he asked.

Then he followed up with, "Do you participate in any homosexual activity? Are you a cocaine user?"

I obviously answered with an emphatic "no" to all those questions; I told him that I had just gone out for one beer the night before.

Then he asked me a question that completely startled me.

"Where did you get this rash from?"

I looked down and all of a sudden, these red spots were forming all over my body as we were speaking. I had never experienced anything like this before.

And the conversation really took a grim tone when he said, "You need to phone your parents right away."

"Why, am I going to die?" I replied in disbelief.

"Yes. You could die in the next hour," the doctor said flatly. "This could stop your heart at any time."

So they stretched the long cord of the phone over to the examining table where I was lying and I had to phone my parents and tell them this awful news. They were living in Vancouver at the time and obviously were not expecting to receive a phone call that their pro hockey-playing son was on the verge of death.

The doctor got on the phone after I broke the news to my parents and he told my mom that he suspected I had meningitis—or meningococcal septicemia. They were going to put me on an aggressive treatment of antibiotics, but there were no guarantees.

From that point forward, the next week or 10 days was a complete blur in the intensive care unit. They had pumped me so full of antibiotics, and my immune system was so weak, that I really don't remember very much at all.

One thing I do vividly recall is my parents walking into the hospital room and seeing me for the first time in this condition. My parents hadn't seen me in about eight or nine months and I had actually grown out my hair during that time. That, coupled with my bloated appearance from the constant stream of intravenous drugs, totally shocked my parents.

"That's not my son," I remember my mom saying when I sat up to greet them for the first time.

But the medical staff assured her that it was me under that long, sweaty hair and swollen face.

It's probably a good thing that I wasn't all that recognizable, because this would have been a very interesting story for the media. An NHL goalie having a near-death experience would have made the front pages of the paper. The hospital was actually worried about me getting harassed, so they moved me into the geriatric ward so that I could be hidden from the public eye.

There were some drawbacks to being placed among senior citizens—most notably one particular crusty and crotchety patient. This old man was so mean and nasty he would routinely throw his bedpan at the nurses while verbally abusing them. I vowed that if I ever regained my strength, I was going to walk over and tell that old buzzard off. My recovery plan didn't even have a return to the NHL on its radar; it was as simple as trying to just get up and walk over to yell at an old man.

Meningitis really takes a toll on your muscular system. I basically had to retrain myself to walk again. I knew how to walk, but my muscles had been decimated by the virus. My brother Dave used to carry me to the shower in my hospital room because I couldn't walk there myself.

Fortunately, because the virus attacked me while I was at the hospital, they were able to treat me quickly and with a high degree of success. After a few weeks, I was able to get my strength back. Once I was mobile again—and able to walk by myself—I paid a visit to that crotchety old patient.

"You start being nice to people, or else I'm going to come back to pay you a visit," I threatened him. A couple of days later, the nurses told me that the old man was actually treating them with a little more respect. I guess I really shook up the old man with my visit.

Once that important step in the rehab process was out of the way, I was able to start thinking about resuming my hockey career. Word had spread around the league that I had contracted meningitis and my playing career was in jeopardy.

The Islanders decided not to offer me a contract that summer, making me a free agent on July 1, 1996.

Fortunately, my agent, Art Breeze, had taken a signed doctor's note to the NHL Draft to tell all the general managers that I was expected to make a full recovery. The St. Louis Blues were not scared off by my medical condition and they offered me a two-year contract. It wasn't a coincidence that the Islanders and Blues had shared an AHL affiliation agreement in Worcester, so the St. Louis organization knew me pretty well. I'm actually quite certain that my old coach Jimmy Roberts had a say in my going there.

In fact, while I was sick in the hospital, I had more calls from the Blues organization to see how I was doing than I had from the Islanders. The only person from the New York front office to call me was Darcy Regier and I will always be grateful for that.

I was able to report to training camp that fall and, despite losing 30 pounds during that whole summer ordeal, I played the entire season in the AHL in Worcester without incident.

The following season, in 1997–98, I made it back to the NHL and played in 30 games for St. Louis. From a statistical standpoint, I had one of my best seasons, winning 16 games, posting two shutouts with a 2.17 GAA. But of course this comeback story went beyond those numbers.

At the conclusion of that season, I was very humbled to be awarded the Bill Masterson Trophy for perseverance and dedication to the game. I never anticipated winning a major award in the NHL, but it certainly meant a lot to me. I felt like it was total closure for the whole meningitis episode and my health would never be questioned again.

I know it's a cliché to say that having a near-death experience really changes your perspective on life, but in my case that is exactly what happened. I was a 25-year-old athlete who had come within one hour of dying and losing it all. From that point forward, I tried to make sure I always enjoyed my life and appreciated the family and friends that have surrounded me.

6

Naked People and Crazy Stories from the Ice

When you're a goalie with a shutout going in a road game, the hostile crowd in the home arena will try anything to break your concentration. One of the most popular methods is to chant your name to try to get under your skin.

"Mc-Lennnn-an...Mc-Lennnn-an" is a chant I often heard in opposing rinks, as fans like to draw out the syllables of your name to really agitate you. I was never bothered by the chanting, because if you're in a zone, there is no chance some loudmouth fans are going to get into your mental kitchen.

But one night in Vancouver a fan tried a very unique way to jinx my shutout bid against the Canucks. I was playing with the Blues on March 9, 1998, and the big story in the NHL that day was that a naked guy had jumped onto the ice in Calgary the previous night. It was all the talk in the dressing room that morning and the media were even asking us questions about what we would do if we were confronted with a naked fan on the ice.

That night in Vancouver, we quickly took a 2–0 lead, chasing their starting goalie, Arturs Irbe. Garth Snow replaced him in the second period and we scored two more goals, giving me a comfortable 4–0 lead in the game. I was in a groove with a shutout going in the third period against the Canucks, who had some decent firepower. My biggest concern was Pavel Bure—the premier sniper in the game— who could ruin my shutout bid with one of his devastating slap shots.

With about 10 minutes to play in the third period, we had a face-off in our zone. Just before linesman Kevin Collins dropped the puck, I noticed something out of the corner of my eye. Coming toward me at full speed was a partially naked fan, who had made his way onto the ice surface near the Canucks bench without anyone seeing him or stopping him. And because the officials and the players were all focused on the impending face-off, I seemed to be the only person on the ice who saw this nut job.

Suddenly, Pavel Bure was not my biggest concern on the ice in Vancouver. What was this guy going to do to me? A million thoughts raced through my mind, but one thing was sure: If he got to me, I was going to clobber this guy with my stick and blocker. I had learned my lesson from Billy Smith years before: Nobody comes into my blue paint—and that includes mascots and crazy naked people.

I started to shout to Collins and the other officials. "Hey, hey, hey!" I yelled at the top of my voice to try to catch their attention. But everybody was so focused on the puck, they weren't paying attention to the bizarre situation unfolding right behind them.

Fortunately for me, one other player on the ice had also noticed the partially naked fan. And it was extra fortunate for me that the player happened to be Enrico Ciccone—Vancouver's resident tough guy, who racked up almost 1,500 minutes in penalties during his career.

Without missing a beat, Ciccone took his stick and hooked this guy by the throat, sending him onto the ice. He slid from the blue line down in my direction, before being tackled by the on-ice officials who had finally clued into the mayhem. I never had to dish out my own brand of vigilante justice to the guy, but I'm sure he was intending to come and visit me in my crease.

For the record, I did keep my shutout that night despite the naked guy's best attempts to foil my bid. Now if they sent a partially naked woman in my direction, I have to admit I may have been a little more distracted.

I wish that was my only story about a naked male fan for this book, but when you play almost 20 years of professional hockey, you're bound to have multiple stories of this nature.

A couple of years later, when I was with the Calgary Flames, we had another naked-guy incident on the ice. This time we were playing against Boston in one of the early games in the regular season on October 17, 2002. Our coach, Greg Gilbert, had made Rob Niedermayer a healthy scratch for this game against the Bruins, a surprising move in the minds of many. Rob was an established NHLer at this point and I believe this was the first time he was ever made a healthy scratch. The buzz going around our dressing room that evening was that Nieds was pissed off about being scratched for this game.

Fast-forward to the third period of this game against the Bruins. We were tied at 3 during the final TV timeout. I was sitting at the end of our bench, listening as usual to the chatter on the bench that goes on during these stoppages in play. Suddenly, I noticed a commotion at the other side of the ice that had captured everyone's attention. There was a man on the glass of the penalty box who had just shed his trench coat and was completely naked—with the exception of a pair of red socks.

This guy was now trying to scale the glass and get onto the ice surface. In the Saddledome, the glass is very high and this guy was in trouble when he reached the top. Apparently, when you are wearing nothing but a pair of socks it's hard to imitate Spiderman climbing a wall. As you might expect, this guy fell right onto the ice surface—but unfortunately for him, he fell head first.

He knocked himself out cold in the process, to the shock of 19,000 fans watching him. Honestly, my initial thought was that he was dead. He was lying on the ice completely motionless, stark naked but for those his red socks. His body had gone completely limp and, because we could see his midsection, we knew that the limpness also extended to his private parts. It was embarrassing and scary all at the same time. Instead of worrying about a 3–3 hockey game with the Boston Bruins, we were all focused on a crazy, naked man who was unconscious on the ice.

Our trainer immediately ran across the ice to try to revive this guy. We started to think that he had broken his neck and couldn't breathe. While we had some sympathy for the guy, we also figured he had to be a moron. I mean, who strips down to nothing but red socks and then jumps onto the ice at an NHL game? And so we stared making some little jokes along the bench, until Scott Nichol skated by with the best form of comic relief.

"Hey, boys, Nieds has hit rock bottom," he said, pointing to the naked guy. "Look at him over there."

We all started laughing on the bench. Nichol had just suggested that Rob Niedermayer had jumped from the press box—stark naked—because he couldn't handle being a healthy scratch. Honestly, it was one of the funniest things I'd ever heard in my life. We knew Nieds was pissed off about being a healthy scratch, so the timing of this joke couldn't have been any better. But now we looked like insensitive jerks because we were laughing so hard while this guy was still receiving medical attention on the ice. Most of us had to pull our jerseys up over our faces to conceal the laughter.

A couple of moments later, it was okay to laugh out in the open because the guy came to his senses. He even started waving to the crowd, so we knew he was going to make a full recovery. Of course part of his recovery would likely take place in a holding cell, since the police were waiting for him at the Zamboni entrance.

I never got a clean look at the guy's face, but I am pretty sure it wasn't Rob Niedermayer who made the jump. For the next couple of weeks, though, I did check to see if he was ever wearing red socks.

Jaroslav Modry and the $800,000 Blocked Shot

While the salary-cap era of hockey has allowed for teams to compete on an even playing field, it has eliminated one interesting element from the game: player bonuses.

In the past, players would receive significant compensation for achieving certain statistical milestones during the course of a season. A goaltender could get an extra $250,000 if he won 30 games or a forward might be the recipient of a $500,000 check if he scored 40 goals.

Negotiating individual bonuses was a big part of contract negotiations, because we could take a little less in base salary if there were enough attainable milestones built into the deal.

Toward the end of the regular season, guys were always talking about their bonuses. It wasn't exactly a dressing-room secret about who needed to reach certain milestones. As a player, you always wanted to help out teammates financially, so if everybody knew that a teammate needed one more goal for an extra $200,000, the forwards would try to pass him the puck as often as possible.

At the end of the 1998–99 season with the St. Louis Blues, we had a number of players who were close to reaching some performance bonuses in their contracts. The nice thing in St. Louis was that Joel Quenneville made sure he was aware of this and tried to coach the team accordingly. When you're having a great season like we were that year, it's a lot easier for the coach to help out with these types of incentives.

We were sitting on the plane one day with a couple of weeks left in the regular season and Coach Q came around and asked each player about his bonus situation. I remember thinking to myself, "I'm close. I need four games for a bonus." But I was too shy to say anything to Coach Q. I had told Prongs about this and, of course, he called Coach Q over to our area and prodded me. "Go on, tell him, Noodles."

"I need four games to get my bonus for playing in 30 games this season," I announced to Coach Q. Joel paused and went through the schedule in his head. "We probably have you penciled in for two games, maybe three. But let me see what I can do for you."

From the seat behind me, Grant Fuhr chimed in: "Don't worry, Noodles, we'll make sure you hit that bonus."

As Joel went around the plane, it came out that a couple of players were very close to reaching performance bonuses. Pavol Demitra, who was having a breakout season, needed just a handful of points to get to 90—and an extra $500,000 would kick in for him. Considering Pavol had never even reached the 60-point plateau before, this was pretty amazing. And we also found out that if Scott Young could get to 25 goals, he would get a performance bonus of $300,000.

We went into the final game of the regular season in Los Angeles with neither team having anything to play for in the standings. Our club had sewn up a playoff spot and the Kings were well out of the race, so there wasn't a lot of intensity to this match-up. It was one of those games where both teams were just hoping to escape without any significant injuries.

The only thing we had left to play for were our individual performance bonuses. Demitra was sitting on 89 points, so he needed just a single point to get his $500,000 bonus. Meanwhile, Scott Young needed two goals to have his $300,000 clause kick in. On the other side, the Kings players also had several guys trying to reach their bonuses, so this game had an interesting side story for the guys on the ice, even though the fans in the stands would have no idea about this subplot.

When the game started, Luc Robitaille started shooting at me from every possible angle. He was shooting from the blue line, the face-off circle—even from behind the net. It was clear that Luc was trying desperately to score a goal for his performance bonus. A quick look at the stat sheet that day showed that Luc was sitting on 39 goals—so the next one was obviously valuable to him.

He even chatted me up during one of the stoppages in play.

"Hey, Noodles, you got to let one in for me," he pleaded—only half-jokingly.

Now I was all for letting teammates reach their performance bonuses, but there was no way I could just allow a goal to an opposing player for the sake of it. The integrity of the game still needs to be remembered, so I joked with Luc that he was going to have to earn his goal the hard way.

Luc ended up having eight shots on me that day—more shots on goal than anyone else on either team.

On our side, Scott Young opened the scoring in the first period—so now he needed just one goal to reach his bonus. Then, in the second period, Demitra set up Lubos Bartecko for a goal—giving him the assist he desperately needed for his $500,000. Pavol was grinning ear to ear, as he was probably thinking about how he would spend that cash. But the referee decided to wave off the goal because Bartecko, he said, had been in the crease.

They went to video review and it showed that part of Bartecko's skate had been inside the blue paint. He wasn't interfering with Stephane Fiset, the Kings goalie, but because the NHL crease rules were so strictly enforced at the time, they had to wave off the goal. So, thanks to Bartecko's skate lace, Pavol had to watch his bonus disappear into thin air. Luckily for him, there was still plenty of time left on the clock.

We traded goals with the Kings in the second period, but nobody with any significant performance bonuses scored. Robitaille was still held off the score-sheet, but Jason Blake did score his first career NHL goal against me that afternoon for Los Angeles.

We had a 3–2 lead with a minute to go in the game, so Larry Robinson pulled his goalie to get the extra attacker on the ice for his Kings. When he saw this, Joel Quenneville realized that he could throw out his guys who needed to score for their performance bonuses, so in the final shift of the game, both Pavol Demitra and Scott Young were on the ice for us.

The puck was in our zone with about 20 seconds left on the clock when it got chipped along the boards. Pavol skated over and poked it ahead of Rob Blake—who basically just let him by with the puck. If this had been a game that meant something in the standings, I know Rob Blake would have flattened Pavol on that play. But I have a feeling that Rob knew our guys were trying desperately to score a goal for their bonuses, so he just let Pavol breeze by him uncontested. These were the dying seconds of the last game of the regular season, so it really didn't matter at that point to Rob.

And now the perfect situation had unfolded: Pavol Demitra had a two-on-one with Scott Young, with the Kings' net empty. If Pavol could slide the puck over to Scott, he could put it into the net and it would be a win-win situation for them. Scott would hit his goal bonus, while Pavol would pick up his much-needed point via an assist.

They crossed the Kings' blue line with about 10 seconds left on the clock and Pavol had a clear path to the net. He could have easily shot the puck into the net and reached his own bonus, without even thinking of Scott. But since he was such a good teammate, Pavol passed up on the free shot at the net and slid the puck over to Scott instead.

And Scott—who had the reputation of having one of the heaviest shots in the NHL—let go of the hardest one-timer I've ever seen come off his stick. This puck wasn't just going to go into the net; it was going to rip the netting apart.

But just as the puck left Young's stick, Kings defenseman Jaroslav Modry came across the ice and blocked the shot out of desperation. This wasn't just an ordinary shot block: Modry actually went down onto the ice and did a double-stack with his shin pads. The puck went off his top leg and over the glass and into the crowd. In one fell swoop, Jaroslav Modry had just taken away $800,000 in performance bonuses from our guys.

The players on the ice for both teams couldn't believe it. Modry—who barely spoke any English—clearly was unaware that this goal meant so much to our guys. Blake had just let them take the puck through the neutral zone because I'm sure he didn't mind if they scored the goal. But Modry obviously hadn't received the memo and made the most ridiculous shot block I had ever seen. It was as if he were trying to stop a goal during Game 7 of a playoff series.

Because the subsequent face-off was back in the Kings' zone, Larry Robinson was forced to put his goalie back into the net. And with only five or six seconds left on the clock, it effectively killed any chance for Pavol and Scott to hit their bonus target. The final buzzer sounded and we were consoling Pavol and Scott as we left the ice.

We nicknamed Modry's play the "$800,000 Blocked Shot" and it quickly became a story that was told inside the Blues dressing room for years to come.

But the story doesn't actually end there. Our general manager, Larry Pleau, was very impressed with what Pavol tried to do on the final play of the game. Larry knew that Pavol could have easily put the puck into the open net and secured the bonus for himself. But instead, he made sure he passed the puck to Scott so that he could try and score the goal.

So, at the end of the season, in one of the classiest moves I've ever seen, Larry decided to pay Pavol half his $500,000 bonus because he felt it was the right thing to do. And I think he even gave Scott a bit of money too for coming so close to his 25-goal bonus.

In the end, I suppose Jaroslav Modry actually cost our guys about $500,000—but we still refer to it as the "$800,000 Blocked Shot" to this day.

The Narcoleptic Trainer

In my rookie year in New York, we had this legendary trainer named Eddie Tyburski.

Eddie was the exact opposite of what you would imagine a trainer to look like. He was anything but the picture of health—he was probably 50 pounds overweight and a chain smoker. I would be on the training table and he would be smoking while working on my back. There would be ashes flying all over the place.

"You know, Noodles, you should be taking better care of yourself," he would tell me, while he alternated puffs of a cigarette and bites of a greasy piece of pizza. I always found it hard to take health and lifestyle advice from a guy who looked like he was the poster boy for high cholesterol.

On top of being overweight, Eddie was also narcoleptic. He would fall asleep almost anywhere. He would always fall asleep on the team bus after a game. We wouldn't even be out of the parking lot in New Jersey and Eddie was dead asleep. And he was one of those active sleepers, so his arms and legs were often flailing around. It was almost comical to see him sitting next to Al Arbour on the bus, dead asleep—but with his arms and legs kicking. On commercial flights, Eddie usually got a couple of seats to himself because nobody wanted to sit next to him.

Falling asleep on a bus or a team plane is one thing. But dozing off during the middle of a hockey game is a completely different matter. Sure enough, it happened to Eddie one night in Long Island.

We were playing a game against the Quebec Nordiques at home. The game was tied 1–1 in the third period. It was probably a bit of a snoozer of a game, but you certainly don't expect to hear somebody snoring behind you on the bench.

I was backing up Ron Hextall that night. Just behind me, I heard the distinct sound of Eddie's snore. He was leaning up against a Gatorade cooler and he was completely passed out. Out of the corner of my eye, I could see Al Arbour at the other end of the bench, staring at Eddie in disbelief. So I tried to get Eddie's attention before the coach came over and tore a strip off him.

"Tyber, Tyber, wake up!" I whispered to him, tapping him with my stick.

But I got no response. The guy was out cold. I'm pretty sure the fans in the second deck of the stands could hear his snoring. Finally I had to yell at him at the top of my lungs—and it woke him up. At that point, I locked eyes with Al Arbour and he knew that I had just woken up our trainer in the middle of the game.

But Al had a lot of patience for Eddie, because for all his shortcomings, he was actually a pretty damn good trainer. In fact, he even helped save Brian Mullen's life.

Brian Mullen had a stroke in 1993 and a lot of people thought his playing days were over. But in the spring of 1994, he was back practicing with us in the hopes of resuming his career.

One day after practice, I was on the ice with a few guys, having an informal three-on-three scrimmage. Brian was taking part in it when suddenly he collapsed on the ice.

I didn't know what to do, so I tried to put my blocker behind his head and clear his windpipe because he was foaming at the mouth. It looked like he was having a seizure right in front of us.

Fortunately, somebody ran into the training room and summoned Eddie—who thankfully was not asleep at the time, but was puffing away on a dart. Eddie ran out onto the ice and helped stabilize Brian Mullen.

A rink attendant got on the phone and dialed 911 and emergency crews showed up to the arena. They took Brian to the hospital via helicopter—that's how serious the situation was. But Eddie played a critical role in helping Brian until the paramedics arrived. If it hadn't been for him, the situation could have played out a lot differently. Tyber was a cool head in a stressful life-and-death situation. I will never forget the moment when an overweight, narcoleptic, chain-smoking trainer stepped up and became a hero.

7

Rookie Dinners and Other Stories That Should Have Landed Me in Jail

As soon as the NHL schedule comes out in the summer, I can guarantee you that the veteran players on each team are planning one thing: When can we have the rookie dinner?

Rookie dinners are one of the great traditions in hockey that have survived the test of time. First-year players are forced to buy dinner for the entire team on one specified night. Veterans often taunt the rookies in the hours leading up to the dinner, threatening to order the most expensive bottle of wine, coupled with a high-end lobster meal. It really is one of the most fun nights of the year—provided you're not the rookie footing the bill.

There are several critical elements to planning the rookie dinner. For example, you need to make sure there is a significant break in the schedule afterward so you will have a couple of days to recover from the ridiculous antics that usually take place. You also want to try to do the rookie dinner in a cool city—like Chicago or New York—so you can really have a good time.

When I was with the Calgary Flames, we had the perfect scenario to pull off the rookie dinner. We were on a road trip with a couple of days off in Chicago and we all decided that would be the best time to have our annual rookie dinner. We figured we would have a day or two to sweat out the excess alcohol in our bodies and get ready to play the Blackhawks.

That Flames team might have been the most close-knit group I was ever part of during my playing career. It just seemed like everybody got along inside that dressing room; there were no cliques or factions that didn't mix with the others. We had some terrific people like Jarome Iginla, Robyn Regehr and Steve Montador, guys that just got along with everyone else. I firmly believe that our off-ice chemistry was a big reason for our success on the ice in Calgary.

But the ultimate "glue" guy inside that room was Rhett Warrener. If you were to look up the word "teammate" in the dictionary, I'm pretty sure there would just be a picture of Rhett. On the ice, the guy was a consummate professional—blocking shots, dropping the gloves and doing whatever it took to win. Off the ice, Rhett was always the one opening up his house for team parties and organizing these unforgettable bonding events. Whenever there was fun to be had, you could pretty much guarantee that Rhett was right in the middle of it all.

So on this particular day in Chicago, as you might expect, Rhett was the central figure in our team's rookie dinner. To get ourselves ready for the big night, we decided to head down to a little pub near the hotel and start warming up for the night ahead. As is often the case, one drink led to seven or eight and suddenly we were a pretty intoxicated group heading to the restaurant.

Once we were inside our private area of the restaurant, Rhett quickly got himself into more comfortable attire. Naturally, this involved him stripping down to his underwear. You have to remember, this was a pretty high-end restaurant in downtown Chicago. Imagine having a nice steak dinner with your wife and getting a peek into a private party room where a guy is roaming around in his boxer shorts. You'd have to do a double-take because it would seem so preposterous. Keep in mind this was pre-YouTube or Twitter days, where a picture can get a person in a whole world of trouble.

And not only was Rhett in his boxer shorts, but we had gathered some props to make him the "King of the Rookie Dinner." We fashioned a crown out of something and had even managed to secure a cape and a faux-wooden staff to give an aura of credibility to his title as king. Rhett was also sitting at the head of the 50-foot-long-table to make him appear as regal as possible.

And you might have thought he was actually royalty—until you remembered that he wasn't wearing any pants.

Rhett was walking around and mingling with everyone, striking up conversations with his wooden staff in one hand and a bottle of Crown Royal in the other. With each sip of Crown Royal, the king's judgment became increasingly impaired—until he finally had a ridiculous idea.

Rhett turned to me and said, "Do you think I should do a table dive?"

I was stunned that he was even contemplating this move, so I tried to talk him out of it. "Listen, I don't think that's a good idea," I told him. "There is a lot of glass on the table and people are just getting their meals served. Not sure this is smart." When I'm the voice of reason, you know things have probably gotten way out of hand.

Dressing up like a fake king and wearing only your underwear is one thing. But taking a running start and diving across a 50-foot table and taking out everyone's dinner and drinks was something completely different. After a lot of coaxing on my part, Rhett assured me that he was not going to go through with his plan.

Comfortable that Rhett wasn't going to do his table dive, I decided to move around the room myself and chat with some of my other teammates. Every now and then, I would glance over at Rhett to make sure he wasn't going to follow through on his insane plan.

But just as I turned my back on him, Rhett made his move.

Before I could stop him, his body was hydroplaning down the long table. Rhett had taken a running start, so he was traveling at a pretty good speed. And while he was going down the table headfirst, he was knocking off everybody's food, drinks and cutlery. There was surf and turf and glasses of wine flying everywhere. It was like Rhett was doing this amazing magic trick where he cleared the table—only not as gracefully as David Copperfield.

To compound the problem, Rhett pulled off this stunt while only wearing his underwear. That meant his entire body was subjected to broken glass, cutlery and other flying debris. When we picked Rhett up off the floor, he was covered in blood. He cut his hand pretty badly and had some other cuts on the inside of his leg. It was pretty obvious to all of us in the room that Rhett needed some medical attention.

"I think I may need a stitch or two," he told me, as blood was firing out of his hand.

"Umm...yeah you do, dummy," I replied sarcastically.

Rhett, however, refused to go to the hospital because he didn't want to ruin everybody's night and put a damper on things. We also were reluctant to call team management and tell them what happened because they probably did not want to hear about how their multi-million dollar asset was doing a near-naked table dive at a fancy steakhouse.

Now we were kind of stuck. How could we get Rhett some medical help without drawing too much attention to ourselves?

Just then, one of the waiters walked up and told us that he had a friend who was a doctor. If we were comfortable with it, he said, he would call him to come over and help out Rhett. This seemed like our best option—although we had no idea if this guy was actually a doctor, a dental hygienist or even a janitor. At that point, we didn't care. We just wanted someone to come over and stitch up Rhett's injuries—and keep it on the down-low.

The waiter's friend arrived on the scene and pulled Rhett into a little area that was just off to the side of the kitchen. Fortunately, this was not the time that the health inspector showed up, because I'm pretty sure that operating a mobile medical station within 20 feet of the kitchen is against the code. Rhett got a few stitches on his hand and some bandages to the little cuts on the inside of his leg. We all ended up pulling together some money and we paid this "doctor" a huge wad of cash to sew up Rhett.

And just like that, we were ready to continue our night. The restaurant staff weren't even upset about the whole incident. In fact, they gave us all free hats to wear for the rest of the night. Rhett was more than happy to trade his fake crown in for a regular ball cap. He'd had enough fun for one night.

I know most hockey fans think of Rhett Warrener as one of the most solid and dependable defensemen. And whenever I think of Rhett, I first remember that he was one of the most fierce and loyal teammates that I ever played with. But of course, I will also remember the guy who went sliding down a table wearing nothing but his boxer shorts and a paper crown. The king was always ready to entertain his subjects and thanks to him, it was probably the most memorable rookie dinner I ever attended.

The Night We Borrowed a Cab in Montreal

If there is one thing NHL coaches detest, it's being forced to spend an extra night on the road in Montreal. Of all the cities in the league, Montreal is the one where players just seem to get into the most trouble.

I know a lot of coaches probably look at the schedule when it first comes out and try to figure out a way to avoid spending extra time in that city. On the flip side, there are a few coaches who use an extra night in Montreal as an incentive: "Win a game tonight and you get to spend an extra evening in Montreal next week."

One of my most unforgettable nights on the road happened to occur in Montreal. But unlike a lot of other memorable stories from players, this one doesn't include the Chez Parée strip club or chasing women in the streets.

This is one of those stories where I feel obligated to conceal the identities of my running mates (or victims) as they had no idea what was in store. I won't tell you what year this happened or what team I was playing with at the time. But I can tell you that I was in the company of several multi-millionaire teammates. I think there were four of us involved and our total salaries probably added up to north of $10 million. My portion of that pie was in the neighborhood north of $500,000—so you can imagine just how high-profile the other guys were. (And before you start throwing out guesses, I can tell you unequivocally that Jarome Iginla is NOT one of the players involved with this story.)

On this particular night, we were on one of those dream road trips for an NHL player that pop up every few years. For some reason, we were in Montreal, but we had a full two days off before our next game on the schedule. This means we had a green light to go out and fully enjoy ourselves on our first night in the city.

Before we went out for a night of fun, the first thing we wanted to do was to go out and grab something to eat. We were trying to ask people about recommendations for a nearby restaurant, but of course there is a bit of a language barrier in Montreal.

So we decided that our best bet would be to hail a taxicab on the street and have the driver take us to a restaurant. We stepped outside of our hotel and immediately flagged down the first cab that drove by.

As we piled into the vehicle, the cabbie seemed a little bit nervous about this situation. He had no way of knowing we were four well-paid professional hockey players. To him, we probably looked like a bunch of frat guys who were about to mess up the inside of his vehicle. So before we could tell him where we wanted to go, he demanded $50 up front— probably as insurance against anything stupid that was about to transpire.

My three teammates piled into the backseat of the vehicle, leaving me to take the front seat and handle negotiations with the driver. As I was about to hand him the cash, I joked to him that I would give him the $50 and an extra $50 on one condition: That I could be the driver.

"No, no, no, you can't do that," he said emphatically.

"Come on, let me just have a little fun this one time," I pleaded.

There was a little bit of back and forth between us and then—to my complete surprise—he relented. The cabbie actually agreed to get out of the car and let me get behind the wheel. He got out of the car on the driver's side and proceeded to walk around the car to get into the passenger seat. At the same time, I quickly slid across to his seat, winked at the boys and took control of the vehicle. And before he could get into the passenger-side door, I stepped on the gas.

That's right: I being the fool I was at that time, "borrowed," in my opinion—a taxicab from its driver.

The cabbie—who was probably thinking the $50 deposit was far from sufficient at this point—started chasing us on foot.

And continuing to be the moron that I was, I would slow down enough for him to get close to the passenger door—before stepping on the gas again. It's like back in high school when you tell a buddy to hop into the car, but you just drive forward every time his hand touches the door handle. Trust me, that joke never gets old and it seems funnier when it's happening under these circumstances.

Once I was in complete control of the situation, I started getting even more cocky behind the wheel. I reached over and flipped the switch on the side of the meter on the dashboard, turning it on. My teammates in the backseat were in hysterics, loving the fact that we'd borrowed a cab and turned on its meter.

I rolled down the side window and yelled back to the cabbie, who was still chasing us on foot: "Come on bud, get in. The meter's running!"

After a few more of the driver's frustrated attempts to open the passenger door, I finally let the poor driver back into his own car. He hopped into the passenger seat with a smile (he was a good sport about it), but he did look relieved just to be back inside his own vehicle. This cab was probably a big part of his life and I was treating it like it was a prop in an elaborate college prank.

This is probably where the story should have ended, but I was still feeling adventurous behind the wheel of the now quasi-stolen taxi cab. Instead of getting out of the vehicle,

I just kept on driving. The driver was so happy to be back in his own car that he was actually trying to help me navigate the streets—turn here, slow down there, he was starting to enjoy this.

But the cabbie's blood pressure started to rise again when I wanted to find out what it was like to drive on the sidewalk. Just like in *Grand Theft Auto*, I started navigating the cab down a vacant sidewalk on an empty street, narrowly missing newspaper boxes, a light pole and I'm sure a few stray boxes. For good measure, I even started driving with no hands on the steering wheel; I managed to find a pair of sunglasses inside the car and put those on, making it look as though I was visually impaired. I believe my final stretch of driving included going the wrong way on a deserted one-way street he had directed us to. On the sidewalk.

My career actually started to flash before my eyes, as I imagined the media getting wind of this story. I could see the headlines: "NHLer McLennan Borrows Cab, Joyrides in Montreal." Not only would I end up in jail and fined, but my playing days might be over as well. If management ever found out about this, I would surely end up being traded or demoted.

And so, finally, common sense got the better of me.

We pulled up close to a restaurant and ended the worst—but probably most entertaining—ride ever for this cabbie. Because he was helping to navigate, deep down I feel part of him enjoyed it. The meter had been running the whole time, so we compensated him for the posted rate—and then some. I think we gave him an extra couple of hundred bucks for his troubles, although I'm not sure that would have covered his subsequent therapy sessions.

I did ask him for a receipt, but he declined. In hindsight, we probably wouldn't want any physical evidence of this night in case the authorities did get involved. The cabbie also declined to join us for dinner, even though I extended the offer. I guess he didn't feel like eating rotisserie chicken with the four men who had just borrowed his vehicle and traumatized him for 15 minutes.

I would never attempt to pull this stunt again, not in my wildest dreams, because as I look back I can see so many serious issues I could have encountered with my stupidity. I have to admit I was very young, foolish and learned a valuable lesson from this—but I also have to admit that it was the beginning of one of the most fun nights I ever had on the road.

The Night I Assaulted a Senior Citizen

In 2009, I made the transition from player to coach, as I was hired by the Calgary Flames to work with the team's goalies.

This was a golden opportunity for me that I couldn't pass up. Getting paid to have Miikka Kiprusoff make me look good—where do I sign up?

Our coaching staff consisted of head coach Brent Sutter, along with assistants Dave Lowry, Ryan McGill and Rob Cookson. We had a great group of guys in the room, many of whom were my former teammates. Since I was moving back to Calgary, I needed a place to live during the season. Fortunately, Mike Keenan—the old head coach in Calgary— had a condo available and I was able to rent it from him for the year. I was even going to have a roommate—my friend Peter Hanlon, who served as the media relations director for the Flames.

On my first night in the new place, I had an unforgettable experience that nearly landed me in jail.

We had spent the day on the golf course, as the team was holding its annual tournament to kick off the regular season. I returned to my new apartment complex in the early evening after a full day on the course. I was so new to the place that I hadn't yet officially registered my vehicle, and I had to park in the visitors' parking lot. The complex had two identical buildings, twin apartment towers that were about 25 stories high.

As I got out of my car, I had to figure out a way to lug all my free swag with me. This was one of those team golf tournaments where each participant was given a whole bunch of free stuff, including a brand new Calgary Flames golf bag. I threw the new golf bag over my shoulder, put my iPod headphones into my ears and headed into the lobby of my apartment building.

With the music cranked in my ears, I headed into the elevator and swiped my key fob to access the 23rd floor for my apartment. I reached my floor and headed to the door with my key in my hand. I tried to open the door, but it didn't seem to work. I fumbled with the lock a couple of times, but the door still wouldn't open.

I started to wonder if Peter was on the other side of the door, messing around with the locks. We often played pranks on each other and this seemed like something that was right up his alley. I still had the music playing in my iPod, so I started pushing on the door and banging on it—assuming Peter would finally just let me inside.

All of a sudden the door to the apartment flew open and there was a man standing there—but it wasn't Peter. It was a senior citizen and he came charging at me full force. He grabbed my shirt and yelled at me, "What are you doing? What are you doing?"

I was completely perplexed by this turn of events and found myself wondering why an old man was inside my apartment. So, as he grabbed me, I made a quick counter-move and threw him onto the floor. It was surprisingly easy to do this—most likely because this man was in his late 60s. Once I had him pinned to the floor, I started choking him and demanding answers.

"Who the fuck are you? Why are you in my apartment? What do you want?"

But the old man was pretty feisty. He was still shouting at me, asking what I was doing at the door. Now I was getting pissed at the old man, who didn't seem to be backing down.

"Are you trying to rob me, old man?" I shouted at him, as I pushed his head against the ground.

Just then a woman appeared at the door and she was screaming at the top of her voice. I now realized that this was a two-person operation; the old man wasn't working alone. The woman was shrieking, "What are you doing?"

I answered with a question that nobody had been able to answer. "Why the fuck are you guys in my apartment? What are you doing here?"

The woman looked at me, perplexed, and said, "Your apartment? This is our apartment!"

I was starting to get really agitated now. "Look, this is my apartment. I just rented it last week. Check the door. It says 2301. That's my place."

She looked at me and said, "2301 in what building? The Smith building or the MacLeod building?"

"I'm 2301 the Smith building," I quickly responded.

"This is the MacLeod building!" she fired back.

At this point, I realized I could probably loosen up on the death grip around grandpa's neck. I was clearly the person in the wrong and I had probably just committed a crime. Just as they had in Montreal while I was driving a stolen taxi, the newspaper headlines started to run through my head:

"Flames Coach Wanted in Connection with Home Invasion" or "McLennan Assaults Senior; Charges Pending."

I couldn't believe what I had just done. I had physically assaulted a senior citizen outside his own apartment after what seemed like a botched break-in attempt. The optics of this whole situation did not look good for me. To make matters worse, everyone in the building was on edge because there had been an unsolved murder in the complex a few months earlier. So you can imagine the fear that must have been running through the old man's heart when he saw me trying to break into his place with a set of golf clubs.

As quickly as possible, I helped the man to his feet and tried to apologize. Everybody was shaken up from the incident, because the tensions had escalated so quickly. It turns out that the key fob that I swiped at the elevator accidentally let me into the other building. Technically, this whole episode wasn't my fault, because the fob should have worked only in my own building.

Of course, this family didn't view it that way. They were extremely upset with me and, looking at their perspective, it was hard to argue. After leaving their apartment, I went downstairs to the manager's office to explain the situation. The superintendent was mortified to hear about this glitch in the security system that had just led to a physical altercation between two condo residents.

I started to feel really bad about this whole ordeal, so after I got back to my apartment—the correct 2301 this time—I went across the street to the liquor store. I purchased a nice bottle of wine and wrote a small note for the family I had just terrorized: "I really apologize for what happened. I hope we never have to see each other like that again. Sincerely, Jamie—from the other 2301."

It was probably the most unique autograph I ever signed—and the only one that ever included an apology.

Never Meet Your Idol: How Gene Simmons Disappointed Me with an Egg Salad Handshake

One of the best perks of being a pro goaltender was the ability to express myself through my mask designs. All the other players on the ice have to conform to pretty strict uniform and helmet regulations, but we goalies have an opportunity to let the fans see a bit of our personal sides.

For most of my NHL career, I wore a tribute to one of my favorite bands—KISS—on my mask in some way, shape or form. Sometimes it was a cartoon version of the band along the side of my mask. Other times it was a more subtle version of the band on the back plate behind my head. Anybody who knew me really understood how much I liked KISS.

I had the opportunity to rub elbows with a lot of Hollywood and music celebrities over the course of my career, but after more than 10 years in the National Hockey League, I still really hadn't met Gene Simmons or any of the KISS band members. I was able to say a quick hello to Gene one time after a concert, but I was never able to actually get some private time with him and have a conversation. Thanks to a pure coincidence, that all changed in the spring of 2006.

I was playing for the Florida Panthers at the time and the city of Miami was hosting an IndyCar event just up the road. The defending champion of the race was Dan Wheldon (the legendary Indy racer who sadly passed away in a tragic crash in October 2011). Dan was in town a few days early, preparing for the race and also shooting a reality TV show in which cameras followed him around.

As part of his reality TV show, he wanted to come down to the rink and shoot pucks against an NHL goalie. I was more than happy to oblige, figuring that my workload behind Roberto Luongo was pretty reduced, so I would take anything I could get. As we were wrapping up our practice session, Dan happened to notice my mask.

"I don't know if you know this, but Gene Simmons is one of the ambassadors for IndyCar racing," he said. "He's going to be at the time trials tomorrow afternoon and the race on Sunday. Would you like to come down and meet him?"

He probably didn't even get partway through his final sentence before I blurted out an emphatic "yes!" A chance to have a chat with Gene Simmons? This was a no-brainer for me.

Dan said he would arrange the meeting through his PR man and all I had to do was show up to the racetrack for the time trials on Saturday afternoon.

I was excited to tell Jen—my girlfriend at the time—who was in Florida visiting me from her home in New York. I told her that I would be taking her to the racetrack and she would also get a chance for this once-in-a-lifetime opportunity.

We showed up at the racetrack and, sure enough, Dan Wheldon's people had arranged the VIP passes for the two of us. This allowed us to go right onto the infield of the oval track, meaning the cars were zooming around us at 200 mph.

We walked up near the pit area and Dan came over to greet us. He took us over to his car and gave us a private tour of his vehicle, just moments before he was going to hit the track for his time trial. Even though I was really looking forward to the meeting with Gene Simmons, I had to admit that I was pretty pumped about being so close to the Indy cars. Seeing Dan and his car gave me a real appreciation for the preparation and bravery involved with his sport.

Just before Dan got into his car to start his work, he told us that his PR guy was waiting around the corner. In a few minutes, he would take us into the VIP tent where Gene Simmons was available to meet us.

I'll never forget walking into that tent and seeing Gene Simmons on the other side. A lot of times when you meet your favorite celebrity or idol, you are often blown away at how small they are in real life. That definitely wasn't the case with Gene; he was almost larger than life. I think he's about 6 foot 4, and he certainly has a way of standing out in a crowd with his distinctive hair.

Gene was over standing by a buffet line, so Dan's PR guy went up and started chatting with Gene's PR guy. I was starting to get pumped, knowing that I was finally going to meet a longtime idol of mine.

The PR guys motioned to Gene and he turned around to head over and meet us. Gene was near the buffet and was just wrapping up his lunch, which appeared to be an egg salad sandwich.

As he started walking closer to us, I was thinking about what I was going to say. I was really excited to tell him about my KISS tribute masks—although I'm sure the PR guys would have tipped him off on that story. But as he got closer to us, I realized he had something smeared all over his face. No, it wasn't the trademark KISS face paint that had made Gene an icon around the globe. Instead, it was the remnants of his egg salad sandwich.

In case you think I was being a little too critical, let me be clear: this wasn't just a little smidge of egg salad on the corner of his lip. There was egg salad all over his face. I think his eyebrows were the only part of his face that were spared from this apparent egg salad explosion.

I turned to Jen and whispered, "What the hell is going on here?"

I had pictured a meeting with Gene Simmons unfolding many different ways in my head over the years. But meeting him inside an IndyCar VIP tent with egg salad smeared all over his face was one scenario that hadn't really occurred to me.

Gene's PR guy—clearly oblivious to the facial condition of his star client—stepped in and started the formal introduction.

"Gene, this is Jamie McLennan. He's the NHL goalie who is a big fan of yours. We had him featured in *Tongue Magazine* a while back."

I extended my hand for a handshake with my idol, but I nearly recoiled in horror. Just before he was about to shake my hand, Gene took his right hand and cleaned off his face. No napkin, no sanitary wipe—just his bare hand doing the work of three paper towels. And with his messy hand, he firmly grasped mine and completed the most disgusting handshake of my life.

"Hi Gene, it's nice to meet you. I'm a really big fan," I said, as Gene pressed his egg salad paw into mine.

A lot of times when you meet your favorite celebrity, you say to your friends, "I will never wash this hand again." But I can't tell you how quickly I wanted to wash my hand after this exchange. It might sound cool to have egg salad from a rock star all over your hand, but let me tell you—it's actually not that exciting. More like unsanitary.

As if this wasn't enough, Gene decided to take this bizarre meeting to another level. Being a typical rock star pervert, he figured it was his right to check out my girlfriend right in front of me. So he started twirling Jen around and blatantly check-ing out her backside, while I was neutralized by his egg salad concoction.

Jen was wearing glasses. Gene wanted to see what she looked like without them, so he took his messy hands and removed her glasses, then put the glasses on himself. In the process of taking off her glasses, he smeared more of his egg salad all over her right lens. He put the glasses back on Jen, although now she couldn't see out of her right eye because the lens was completely smudged with egg salad.

Gene simply said, "It was really nice to meet you." And then he just turned around and walked away. My long-awaited meeting had finished in the span of a couple of minutes and had left us both coated in egg salad.

I turned to Jen, who now looked like some sort of bizarre pirate with just one eye.

"What the hell was that?" I said in disbelief. "That was one of my idols? That was Gene Simmons?"

It was the most bizarre celebrity encounter I've ever had in my life. And the way that Gene treated us made me rethink my allegiance to KISS. In fact, when I went back to the rink the next day, I told my trainer it was time for a new mask. I decided to put Nickelback on my mask, retiring the KISS mask forever.

I suppose the moral of the story is: Sometimes it's best not to meet your idol. You might end up extremely disappointed and covered in egg salad.

Hitching a Ride With Chad Kroeger

After my run-in with Gene Simmons, I decided I was done with him and KISS. I went full-time to showing respect to a band where I had friends and I liked their music.

I had become a fan of Nickelback a few years earlier and since they were a Canadian band I figured that it would be a good idea to throw a shout-out to them on my masks. Chad Kroeger and the band are huge hockey fans, so when they saw their band name on my masks, mixed in with KISS before, they got in touch with me. Chad and I have a lot in common. We have the same sense of humor and we like to go out and have fun, so we pretty much had an instant connection.

Of course our schedules didn't always match up when I was a player, because we would often be on the road in different cities across North America. And Nickelback's touring schedule took them all over the world as well. So whenever Chad and I had a chance to hang out, we took advantage of it.

I remember sitting at home one day in Edmonton during the summer and getting a text from Chad. He was doing the MuchMusic Video Awards for the next three days and he wanted to know if I could come to Toronto and hang out. It sounded like it was going to be a sweet gig for him. They just had to play one song at the awards show and they would have the rest of the time off. Chad said there were going to be festivities all weekend and I should come out there.

It wasn't a difficult decision for me: A weekend in Edmonton or three days partying with some rock stars in Toronto?

I was on a plane the next morning and hooked up with the band as they did their rehearsal. I was able to stand onstage as they were performing "Burn It to the Ground" and Chad was even goofing around and changing some of the lyrics to include my name—funny stuff—while he played.

After the rehearsal, we went out for dinner and then we had to appear at a club in Toronto where the owner was paying Chad to make a personal appearance. When we got there, they put us in the middle of the club and Chad was like the main attraction in a petting zoo. There were hundreds of people all around us and everybody wanted to come up and get a piece of Chad.

By this point, I had consumed quite a few drinks and figured I would help the security people keep the fans away. I was sort of pushing people back to make sure they didn't get too close to Chad, plus there was a surge of people just pushing their way into the middle. It was getting scary. Then one really strange-looking woman, with bizarre hair and makeup, came pushing her way up to Chad. I jumped in and pushed her away.

"Beat it, you troll," I said to this circus freak.

After she walked away, Chad turned to me and said, "Did you know that girl you just called a troll was Lady Gaga?"

"Uh-oh . . . that's not good," I replied, feeling pretty embarrassed.

In my defense, she was bombing her way up to Chad in a really weird way, but her security team must have cleared a path for her—an oversight on my part. And this was just before Lady Gaga blew up and become a global phenomenon; I'm pretty sure I wouldn't call her a troll if I ran into her today. Actually, a good rule of thumb is you should never call anyone a troll, but again I clearly wasn't of sound mind that night.

Now, after we got out of the bar, Chad invited a bunch of people back to his hotel. This hotel was not like anything I had ever seen before—and I had stayed in a lot of five-star hotels in my life. They had given Chad a 6,000-square-foot place, which included three separate levels and a top-floor bar and hot tub. If you're going to party like a rock star, you can't do it at the Best Western.

There were tons of people at this party, but there was enough room that it didn't feel crowded. I ended up hanging out with a manager of the band and a couple of other people in one of the bedrooms. It was all pretty mild, just a few people having some drinks, sharing stories and telling jokes.

All of a sudden, on the other side of the room, a "girl fight" breaks out. And this wasn't a girl fight where they slap each other a couple of times. These two women were going at it hard, pulling each other's hair as if they were in a tug-of-war competition.

I decided to step in and try to break up this fight because it was getting nasty. I tried to karate-chop their hands so they would be separated. One of these women had been in the hot tub upstairs and during the course of the fight, her towel fell off—exposing her top half. And no matter what the situation, it's hard not to stare like a 12-year-old boy when a woman loses her top.

I couldn't get them apart, until one woman finally pulled out a chunk of the other one's hair. And I mean it was a big chunk; this woman lost so much hair that she looked like Fire Marshall Bill from the old *In Living Color* show—there was actually blood coming out of her scalp. And the other woman was standing there with a big chunk of hair in her hand, holding it as if she had just caught a prized fish.

The now semi-hairless woman yelled, "I'm a model and I'm going to sue you. I'm calling the police!"

At that point, my alarm bells went off. I was pretty sure Nickelback didn't need the publicity of having the police come and break up one of their parties. So I told them both to calm down, and we ended up kicking out the hair-puller. The other woman was crying, saying, "I've got a modeling shoot coming up. Now I've got no hair and she pulled out my extensions."

I went upstairs to get Chad, who had no idea this just happened, to let him know that this woman was thinking about calling the police and pressing charges. We talked to her and ended up giving her $500 or $600 so she could go and get her hair fixed. Thankfully, we were able to keep the police out of it—but I always enjoy telling the story about how I broke up a girl fight in a rock star's bedroom.

My other favorite story with Chad also involved a late-night party, this time in Vancouver.

We were out to play the Canucks one September during pre-season and Chad wanted to hang out after the game. I think I played a period that night and when we finished at the rink I went down to the Roxy to meet up with Chad.

I told Chad that I had to make sure it wasn't a really late night because I had to be on the team bus at 12 noon. We were flying back home and I could not miss the team charter. I was prepared to have a few drinks, but I wanted to make sure I did not put that flight in jeopardy.

As is often the case at the Roxy, 4:00 a.m. came around very quickly and I was feeling great. Chad said he was inviting a few people back to his place to keep the party going and I was more than welcome to join. He had a limo waiting outside and he told me to come along for the ride.

I foolishly accepted, because Chad actually lives 45 minutes outside Vancouver. But at that point, I didn't really care. I just told the limo driver to make sure he woke me up by 10:00 a.m., because I needed to get back to our team hotel by 11:00 a.m. to pack up and get on the bus.

We got to Chad's place and had a terrific time, goofing around in his house. He's got an indoor rink underneath his house that he built. It's quite amazing; half the size of a regulation arena, complete with a little Zamboni and viewing area, so you can imagine how much fun that would be after a few drinks. We played some hockey, then hung out by the pool and had some more drinks, and at some point I found a bedroom and went to sleep.

I felt someone waking me up. It was the limo driver with some bad news.

"Dude, it's 11 a.m.—you're never going to make that team bus."

I was starting to panic a little bit, so I found Chad to explain the situation. He had a typical rock-star solution to my problem.

"Don't worry, pal," he said. "I'll get you a helicopter."

So Chad made a couple of phone calls and, within minutes, there was a helicopter landing on his front lawn. My clothes were all crumpled and my hair was a mess, but I jumped onto this chopper without worrying about my outward appearance.

The helicopter took exactly seven minutes to get from Chad's house to the landing pad near downtown Vancouver. There was a limo waiting to pick me up when I landed and it took me to the hotel. I grabbed all my stuff, crammed it into my suitcase and made it onto the team bus—with about five minutes to spare. If I hadn't had that helicopter, I would never have made it and I would have been in big trouble with the organization.

It's always nice to have friends in high places who can hook you up with a helicopter when you need one.

8

The Slashing Incident and Career Wrap-up

Throughout the course of my pro hockey career, I was known as a pretty laid-back, but talkative player. Unfortunately for me, my legacy was somewhat tainted by my final game in the National Hockey League.

People have often asked me to explain the Johan Franzen incident and there was no way I could leave that episode out of this book. While it was the most embarrassing moment of my career, I feel it's important to explain my thought process during that ugly incident.

It was Game 5 of the Flames' first-round playoff series with the Red Wings in 2007. The series was tied 2–2, but Detroit had complete command in the fifth game of this series on their home ice. They had a 5–1 lead in the third period and the game had been extremely physical. We didn't like the fact that two of their star players—Tomas Holmstrom and Johan Franzen—were taking liberties with Miikka Kiprusoff.

Over the course of a playoff series, the animosity level between two teams gets ratcheted up. Throughout that entire series, we felt like Holmstrom and Franzen were crossing the line when it came to contact with Miikka. Both Holmstrom and Franzen understood that if you wanted to beat an elite goaltender, you needed to get inside his grill. So they would "accidentally" fall on Miikka, but it was pretty obvious to us that it was intentional (or as I call it, "accidentally on purpose"). These two guys were—and still are—among the best in the business of making a living inside the blue paint, so they would rarely get called for goaltender interference or roughing. And by the fifth game of the series, we had had enough of their antics.

So with the Red Wings leading the game 5–1, with less than five minutes left in the third period, our coach, Jim Playfair, decided it was time to pull Miikka out of the nets. He didn't want to expose Kipper to any more Red Wings goals—and he also wanted to make sure he didn't face any more abuse at the hands of Holmstrom and Franzen. By getting him out of the net now, he figured he could get Kipper to start thinking about a must-win Game 6 back on our home ice.

The game had involved several nasty incidents already and Jimmy did not want to have anything happen to Miikka in a game that was no longer winnable. Brett Lebda had submarined Daymond Langkow with a dirty hit at the knees, which sent both players to the ice in pain. Daymond was so upset with Lebda that he crawled over to him and punched him square in the face. A few minutes later, Jarome Iginla got into it with Mathieu Schneider and they battled—and when Jarome is at his best, he's physical and he's nasty. On this day, the Red Wings had irked him and it was clear that the final few minutes of this game were going to be nasty and bloody.

At this point, I was summoned by Jimmy to go in and replace Kipper. A lot of people think that when Jimmy told me to go into the game, he also instructed me to go after Holmstrom or Franzen. I can honestly tell you that no conversation like that ever happened on the bench. Jimmy just wanted me to go in and mop up the rest of the game; he certainly didn't expect me to start something with the Red Wings.

But I was pretty fired up when I headed into the nets. This was my first taste of playoff action in this series, and for the past 10 days I had watched Kipper get abused by the Red Wings. And while Jimmy didn't instruct me to do anything, I wanted to go in there and make a statement for our team. I figured maybe I could give our team a little bit of momentum heading into Game 6 if I could fire up the troops a little bit. It was

Miikka's job to be cool and calm in the crease, but I had a chance to deliver a message to the Red Wings.

And that's where I made my critical mistake. I let my emotions get the best of me and that's always a fatal flaw in playoff hockey. The teams that are the most successful are the ones with players who can handle their emotions in the big game. You need to be able to play with a controlled aggression in the Stanley Cup playoffs.

As the play started, sure enough Johan Franzen was parked right in front of me during a Red Wings attack in our zone. And I started hacking at him. Marc Joanette, the referee, was warning me, "Jamie, don't do that. Knock it off." But I ignored his words and kept slashing the back of Franzen's legs. Finally, Joanette had no choice but to call a penalty on me.

But what really agitated me was that Franzen took his stick and gave me one of those accidental/on-purpose shots to the head—which is a classic veteran move. I figured at that point it was game-on. Franzen was a big boy and he'd just hit me in the head with his stick. I assumed that he was going to come at me right there, on the spot. They don't call Franzen "The Mule" for nothing. He is a large human being and I figured he was at least going to give me a shot to the head and deservedly so.

The play still hadn't been whistled down on the delayed penalty because we hadn't touched the puck. At that point, Franzen skated away because the puck left our zone—but I knew we weren't finished. As the puck was shot back into our zone, I went behind the net to touch it. As soon as I stopped the puck, the referee blew the whistle to call the penalty on me for slashing.

As I looked up, I saw Franzen skating directly at me. I assumed he was coming over to finish up our battle from a few moments earlier. And, given the way he was coming at me, I assumed he was going to punch me right in the mask. I know some people might not believe me, but that's what I was honestly thinking in that situation.

So as Franzen came toward me, I choked up on my goal stick and gave him a two-handed slash to his midsection—where I hit his pants. In my mind, it was a move made out of self-defense (or defense by offense) because I was certain he was coming to fight me. But I understand the optics of it, because it looks absolutely terrible when you see the replay on television. It looks like I just went after Franzen with a slash for no apparent reason.

Now if I'd really wanted to hurt Franzen, I would have delivered that blow to his upper body near his head, which is why I slashed him on the leg of his pants—not that it makes it any better. And while Franzen went down immediately, he was never in any serious pain. In fact, I remember reading a quote from him in the newspaper the next day in which he said he was more surprised than hurt on the play.

But the fact of the matter is, I was completely in the wrong. I had embarrassed my teammates, the organization and the entire National Hockey League. To add to the mess, this was an afternoon game being broadcast across the United States on NBC, so my antics would not fly under the radar.

If you listen to the broadcasters who were calling that game, they were absolutely stunned with what had transpired. As I said, I never had the reputation of being one of the goalies who would use my stick as a weapon. "That is so out of character for him—that's bizarre," said NBC analyst Pierre McGuire at the time that it happened.

As I left the ice that day, I was embarrassed—even humiliated. The fans threw some debris at me as I was escorted off the ice, down the visitors' tunnel at Joe Louis Arena. My statistical line from that day was very embarrassing: 18 seconds played, 0 saves, 17 minutes in penalties—not a proud moment whatsoever. They assessed me two minutes for the original slash on Franzen, another five for the baseball swing and then a game misconduct on top of it all. I also made things difficult for Miikka, who had to come back into the game and play the final 2:59. I only ended up giving him an 18-second mental break.

As soon as the game ended, I sent an apology over to the Red Wings dressing room, because I wanted the message relayed to Franzen that I never intended to hurt him in that manner. But at that point, the damage had already been done. I knew I was going to face discipline from the league.

When we got back to Calgary after the game, I couldn't sleep at all that night. I was feeling so sad and awful that I had done such a terrible thing on such a big stage. This was the NHL playoffs between Detroit and Calgary and I wasn't even supposed to be part of this series—let alone a significant factor. But through my foolishness, I had inserted myself into the storyline in a very regrettable way.

The next day I had a conference call with Colin Campbell, who told me that the league had decided to suspend me for my slash on Franzen. There really wasn't anything I could say in my defense. No camera angle was going to make the incident look any better.

The league decided to give me a five-game suspension for the slash and the irony is that I'm still technically serving that suspension today. That game in Detroit was my last ever in the NHL. I'm one of the few guys in NHL history who can say I retired while being suspended—but it's not something I'm proud of. If I ever do make a comeback to the NHL, I'll still owe them four games on that suspension before I can play again.

And for those people wondering, I sent an apology over to Johan right away and have followed his career because I know what type of player he is—a hard, whistle-to-whistle player. I'm glad that he didn't seriously get hurt in the incident, because he has become one of the most consistent playoff performers of his generation.

In fact, the hockey gods made sure that we felt the karma from this incident, because Franzen actually scored the game-winner in overtime of Game 6 of our series that year to eliminate us.

I absolutely regret what happened that afternoon in Detroit and if I could do it all over again, there's no way I would even dream of slashing Johan Franzen.

But I do realize it's something I have to live with for the rest of my life. My only hope is that fans and players remember me for all the positive stuff—and not the one negative incident of my career.

A Few Weeks in the KHL

After my final season with the Calgary Flames in 2006–07, I decided to take a shot at playing overseas to wrap up my playing career.

I had always joked with my European teammates over the years that once I was done playing over here I would go over to their side of the ocean for one season, float around and party it up like I didn't have a care in the world. It always amazed me how the European players came over to North America, danced and partied around in their own unique way, seemingly without an ounce of worry; they loved life. I vowed that I would finish off my career in the same fashion, by going to a foreign country and just having a blast.

At the end of the summer, I was able to sign a contract with Metallurg Magnitogorsk of the Kontinental Hockey League in

Russia. They are one of the better-known teams in the KHL, having launched the career of Pittsburgh Penguins superstar Evgeni Malkin. But despite their fame within the KHL, the club was based in a relatively isolated location. Magnitogorsk is a mining and industrial city located about 850 miles southeast from Moscow on the northern border of Kazakhstan. Unfortunately for me, there were no Borat sightings to be found. Moscow was beautiful, home of the arts, culture and entertainment, but it seemed like it belonged to a different world than Magnitogorsk. As I did my research on the city, I was a little bit leery about traveling to a place that probably wouldn't offer any of the cultural experiences of a city like Moscow. I wasn't sure how much exploring or adventurous traveling I could do in a city that is heavily invested in the steel industry and is known as one of the most polluted cities in the world.

Nonetheless, I packed up my gear, said goodbye to my family and friends and headed out to meet my new teammates in Germany, where they were conducting training camp. The team was staying in a beautiful town called Garmisch, which reminded me a lot of Banff and Jasper back home.

I didn't have much time to enjoy the mountainous scenery, though, because the club was conducting a series of rigorous workouts. In the NHL, the longest on-ice sessions during training camp usually last about 90 minutes. After that, you might have another 30 minutes of off-ice training and stretching.

But here in the KHL, these guys were doing ridiculous six-hour training sessions. I was 36 years old at this point, in the middle of summer, looking to coast through my final season by playing in a great league while having some fun. I was not looking for a series of workouts that could prepare me for the Olympics.

At the end of each day, I was completely wiped out and exhausted. After the final day of training, all the guys were looking to go out and have one memorable night in Garmisch. But I honestly had nothing left in the tank—which is really saying something. People who know me will realize that I must have been really worn out if I was too tired to go out and be social.

I was also not looking forward to the next day's travel schedule. We had a 3:30 a.m. bus to the airport to start the day-long trip to Magnitogorsk, because, as you might imagine, there aren't a lot of direct flights between Garmisch and Magnitogorsk. We had a circular route, which included a bus to Munich, then a flight to Moscow, followed by a long bus ride to another airport and then finally a flight to my new home. All told, this journey was going to take about 20 hours— just another reason why I didn't want to go out drinking and smoking with my new Russian comrades the night before.

I ended up getting a decent sleep, but when I boarded the bus at 3:30 a.m., I realized I was pretty much the only one who had gotten any rest. The rest of the team was completely hammered and it wasn't just my teammates who were into the booze. I'm talking about almost all the coaches whose names I didn't know, so I had given them my own nicknames. Like our assistant coach, whom I called "Tomato Head" because his face was so red it looked like it was going to pop right off his neck. Then there was "Dr. No Sleeves," who was apparently our team doctor but somehow didn't own a single piece of clothing that wasn't a muscle shirt. I referred to our goalie coach as "Stalin" because he was an angry little man who would get into the vodka in the afternoon before our last practice and yell at me in Russian, giving me useless tips about two-pad stacks and skate saves—stuff that had made him successful in his day in the 1970s. Even the freaking interpreter was completely hammered out of his mind, and a lot of the guys were smoking on the bus as well.

We took the bus ride out to the Munich airport. When we got off the bus, I quickly realized how different life would be over here compared to the NHL. Back home, we never worried about our equipment when we traveled on the road. We would leave our equipment at the rink, the trainers would pack it up for us and it would magically appear in our dressing room stall the next day in our new city. The only thing we ever really carried was a small carry-on or suit bag.

Here, I realized, I would be handling all my own luggage. They just handed me my boarding pass and said, "We'll see you on the plane." And since I was coming over from Canada, I had multiple suitcases, my equipment bag and about 24 sticks.

It was pretty tough to load all of that stuff on one cart and maneuver my way around a busy airport.

After I checked in at the Lufthansa kiosk, I made my way through security and boarded the plane. I looked at my watch and realized that we were quite delayed. Our flight was supposed to leave at 7:30 a.m., but now it was at least an hour past that scheduled departure. As I looked to the front of the plane, I realized why we were just sitting on the tarmac, delayed: My new teammates had purchased everything from the duty-free store inside the airport and they were trying to sort out the whole situation. And when I say they'd purchased everything from inside the duty-free store, I'm honestly not exaggerating. Every bottle of liquor and every oversized box of cigarettes had been scooped up by my new teammates.

The worst part was, most of these guys were still completely drunk from the night before. One of the guys was actually trying to light up one of his new duty-free cigarettes on the plane, before he was scolded by a flight attendant. This was quite the welcome to overseas hockey for me—and it was only the beginning.

I had the last seat on the plane, crammed into the final row next to the bathroom. Unfortunately, that gave me a terrific vantage point to hear one of my hungover teammates puking his guts out inside the tiny stall.

The plane ride was horrendous as we hit turbulence and storms the whole way to Moscow. Now that can happen in any area of the world, as planes have to fly through storms and turbulence every day. This was just another case of that, but it seemed to be magnified fivefold because I didn't have a grasp on the language and what everyone was saying around me. And I have to be honest that not a day goes by that I don't think about the friends I lost in the plane crash that claimed the lives of the Lokomotiv Yaroslavl team in September 2011. I did experience a few very scary flights over there, and often wonder if it could have been me that dreadful day. I will never forget the people who perished, some of whom were close friends that I will acknowledge later, but pray that their deaths weren't in vain. Maybe a better form of flight safety will be mandated so the hockey world—and the world in general— never has to lose great people for what might be something that is completely avoidable.

Miraculously, our pilot managed to land the plane safely in Moscow. I was so relieved to be on the ground safely that I wasn't too bothered by the ridiculous situation at customs. Back in North America, almost any customs area is very well organized and efficient. There are well-marked lines, multiple customs agents and it's a fairly seamless process. But over in Moscow, as some might expect, it was a complete Gong Show. There were just two customs agents at a single desk and there was no defined lineup or sense of organization. Somehow, the 35-degree heat and incessant buzz of blackflies was the perfect backdrop to this chaotic scene.

It took me more than two hours to get through the line and it was almost as grueling as one of our six-hour training sessions in Germany. I was completely covered in sweat and exhausted from the customs ordeal.

My equipment and suitcases were waiting for me on the baggage carousel—nobody from the team had picked them up. I was the last guy through the lineup, but fortunately the team actually waited for me.

I managed to board our team bus, which was an ordeal in itself. The loading area for buses at the Moscow airport was about as well-defined and clear as the customs area. There were buses pointed in every possible direction, with no clear signs to indicate which bus was headed to what location.

As I stepped onto the bus, it was like a repeat of our 3:30 a.m. bus in Germany; everybody was smoking and drinking again. It didn't matter what time of day it was, these guys treated bus trips like it was happy hour.

The engine of the bus turned over and we were getting set to start the next leg of our marathon journey to another air-port, which I was told would take between two and five hours to reach, depending on traffic. Of course, there was a problem: A white Toyota Corolla was parked directly behind our bus, making it impossible for our driver to leave the area.

The driver inside the Toyota was honking and getting angry at our bus driver and the bus driver was honking back at him and pretty soon they were engaged in a pretty heated verbal exchange. I didn't understand what they were saying to each other, but I could tell this was not headed in the right direction.

Sure enough, the driver of the Toyota became so enraged that he left his vehicle and came around his car toward our bus driver. He approached the driver's side window and I realized that he was holding something in his hand. I'd seen enough Jason Bourne movies to know that he was carrying a GLOCK—a Russian pistol.

I started yelling, "He's got a gun! He's got a gun!"

The Toyota driver put the handgun right into our driver's face as they continued their intense argument. To my complete surprise, our driver didn't back down at all—despite the fact that this man seemed to be willing to play a game of "Russian" roulette.

The tensions continued to rise. Still freaked out by the whole thing, I kept yelling, "Gun! Gun! He's got a gun!"

I looked around and my teammates were acting as if we'd just stopped at a red light. In fact, Nikolai Kulemin, who now plays for the Toronto Maple Leafs, was sitting in front of me on the bus and he was on his cell phone. He turned around and gave me a look as if to say, "Shut up, can't you see I'm on the phone here?" He didn't even flinch at the argument involving a gun that was going on five rows ahead of us. Everyone was drinking and smoking, paying no attention to the life-and-death struggle at the front. The card players beside me didn't even stop their deal or break stride to see what was going on.

After a couple of minutes, the man with the gun backed off, got into his Toyota and sped away. Our bus was now able to pull out and, thankfully, not a single drop of blood had been shed.

I was still shaking with shock and amazement at the scene that had just unfolded in front of my eyes. I was even more astonished by the lack of interest from my teammates. I turned to our captain, Vladislav Boulin, who was one of the only English-speaking players on the team, to see if he had an explanation for this indifference.

"Buly, what's going on? That guy had a gun. Weren't you guys scared?" I asked.

He just looked at me and said, "Hey, man, it's Russia. Everybody has a gun. This is like the Wild West."

At that point, I realized maybe I wasn't cut out for Russia. After just a few minutes in the country, I was completely scared and out of my element. I would like to say that's the only reason I lasted just six weeks in Russia, but there were many factors in my departing quickly, including that they didn't love me either. It was a good and bad experience all rolled into one and I wouldn't give it up for anything.

My First Night on Television

When you spend your whole life as a goaltender, you tend to have a very negative association with a red light. Every time a goal is scored against you, a flashing red light lets everyone in the arena know that you have screwed up. So it's amazing to see how many retired goalies actually seek out the red light of the camera—with a career in television.

Darren Pang, Kelly Hrudey, Kevin Weekes and Glenn Healy are just a few of the many former goaltenders who have become recognizable faces on television in North America. Like those guys, I had a reputation for being a somewhat friendly and colorful goalie when I was an active player, so I figured it might be neat to get an opportunity to work in television sometime.

In the spring of 2011, I got an opportunity to try TV with a chance to be a guest analyst on the TSN hockey panel during the Stanley Cup playoffs. James Duthie—the ultra-smooth host—was the ringleader for a panel that included me, Bob McKenzie and Craig MacTavish.

I have to admit I was pretty nervous about the whole experience, which may sound funny coming from someone who was used to playing in front of 19,000 fans and being a part of that atmosphere. But as a goalie you can hide behind the mask and nobody can really see your facial expressions or any nervous tendencies. Live television—especially in the high-definition world—is a completely different animal. Not only can viewers at home see if you're nervous, they can actually count the individual sweat beads on your forehead if they have a 47-inch television.

Prior to our first live hit that night, we had a production meeting in the late afternoon. Production meetings are very helpful for television rookies, because they almost serve as a dress rehearsal. The on-air talent has a chance to go over the topics for the night with the producers and everyone gets a pretty good sense of what is going to happen once the camera starts rolling.

I felt pretty good during the meeting, but as soon as it ended I was overcome with a feeling of nausea and queasiness. I was starting to think about all the people who might be watching me that night and picking apart my every sentence. Some of these playoff games on TSN attracted well over a million viewers, which didn't exactly help to calm my nerves.

It also didn't help that I had eaten an early lunch that day, so my stomach was full of nervous juices and a sandwich platter. I started to get the nervous sweats and then the feeling of panic—like I needed to throw up. There is one bathroom—with a single stall—located just across the hall from the studio.

I entered the bathroom, wearing my full suit and make-up, since we were supposed to be ready to go on the set shortly. I figured if I could puke, I would feel a whole lot better. I leaned over the toilet and hurled—being careful not to get anything on my tie or dress pants.

I was starting to feel better when I got a glimpse of myself in the mirror. During my vomiting episode, I must have started to sweat profusely because my makeup had started to run along my face. It wasn't too bad, so I dabbed a paper towel around my eyes and cheeks to make sure the make-up didn't look caked on and lumpy.

I was starting to feel a lot better now that I had vomited, cleaned up my face and seemingly pulled myself together. I was feeling calm and relaxed—like I belonged there on television. I even started practicing some of my lines in the mirror, just making sure I had the right timing.

Everything was going well until I made a terrible mistake.

Without even thinking, I took the couple of pieces of paper towel I had used to clean my face, tossed them into the toilet and flushed. But as most clear-thinking people know, paper towel doesn't really flush down the toilet all that well.

So when I flushed the toilet, it made a funny gurgling sound and started to back up. The water was rising instead of flushing—filled with my unappealing concoction of paper towels and vomit. I didn't know what to do. There was no plunger available next to the toilet and I was beginning to panic. I was envisioning the different scenarios for how this was going to play out (in fact, I think at that moment I was asking God for some sort of miracle) when I heard the doorknob being rattled. Someone was trying to come into the bathroom. It was Bob McKenzie, who I'm sure was looking to come in for some last-second touchups to his makeup and wardrobe before he went onto the set.

I tried flushing the toilet again, but the water kept rising and now I was worried it was going to flood the bathroom floor. Do I reach my hand in and pull out the paper towel? That didn't seem to be the best way to make friends on the TSN panel. I was pretty sure James Duthie wouldn't appreciate the stench coming from his rookie panelist, whose right hand was soaked with the pungent odor of vomit.

Fortunately, I did notice there was a random stick next to the toilet. It wasn't a plunger or a cleaning brush, but it was a lightning rod from heaven as far as I was concerned and it would have to do in this situation. I took the stick and tried pushing everything back down the toilet. At the last second, my prayers were answered with a distinctive *whoosh* sound. The toilet had miraculously flushed and I would avoid the embarrassment of having flooded the TSN bathroom in the minutes leading up to my television debut.

As I came out of the bathroom, Bob gave me an odd look. I guess the whole toilet-clogging episode had worked me into quite a sweat, because my forehead was dripping again and I must have looked pretty nervous. I'm sure Bob just chalked it up to me being anxious about my first time on live television on TSN.

Little did he know that I was actually more nervous about clogging the toilet than going on television. If I had clogged that toilet, I would never have lived that down from the guys at TSN.

And I'm sure they would have relayed that story to every rookie who finished his debut at TSN: "Hey, your first day wasn't so bad. At least you didn't clog the toilet like Noodles."

A Final Note: Saying Goodbye

Over the course of this book, I've shared a lot of funny and lighthearted moments from the world of professional hockey. However, I would be remiss if I didn't take the opportunity to honor the many teammates and friends who have been tragically lost during my time in the game.

When I first heard news of a crash involving a KHL team plane in September 2011, my thoughts raced to all the players and coaches I knew who were playing over in Russia. Sadly, it turned out that six people I knew very well were killed in that accident. There was Pavol Demitra, my old teammate and friend from St. Louis, whom I talked about in the $800,000 blocked-shot story in this book. Brad McCrimmon was a friend and always a great mentor to any of the young Calgary Flames players, given his ties to that organization. I also lost former teammates Karel Rachunek, Alexander Karpovtsev, Igor Korolev and Jan Marek. In one terrible afternoon, the lives of so many families changed forever.

That summer of 2011 was so tragic for the hockey community, as we also lost Wade Belak, Derek Boogaard and Rick Rypien. Those deaths reminded me of the tragic passing of another of my former teammates, Sergei Zholtok, who died unexpectedly at the age of 31 in 2004. As much as the hockey world has given us, it seems equally cruel that so many players have said goodbye too soon.

But for me, there is one loss that had the most profound impact on my life. In the summer of 2009, I experienced the worst phone call that anyone could receive. I was informed that my best friend, Dale Masson, had passed away suddenly at the age of 36. To say that it was unexpected is the biggest understatement you can imagine. Dale was in great shape at the time and sadly passed away while running his relay portion of the Kananaskis 100-mile relay road race. What made this story more heartbreaking is that Dale's wife, Tanya, and their two young sons—Samuel Lewis and Wyatt Jamie (I was so proud that his first son's middle name was in honor of me)—were waiting at the finish line and witnessed him suddenly collapse.

I had spoken to Dale on the phone the night before and there was no indication that anything was wrong. He was teasing me about the usual things we bugged each other about, me with the size of his head and him firing back about the giant Jay Leno chin he felt I was acquiring. We always bantered about everything in life; he was a smart guy, someone I relied on for advice and perspective about any and every facet of life.

In the weeks and months after Dale's death, I spent a lot of time reflecting on the relationship with the best friend I called "Mace."

I first met Mace when we were both teenagers in junior hockey coaching at Bill Ranford's goalie school in Sylvan Lake. We had an instant bond, as we were both goalies from the Edmonton area and we loved to have fun once we took off our pads. He was playing his junior hockey with the Kamloops Blazers while I was just breaking into the professional ranks with the New York Islanders. In the off-season we were inseparable. He was a big part of the crew of guys that would go on the pub crawls and Las Vegas trips every summer.

Mace was always the life of the party when the boys got together. He had charisma and personality that just drew people to him. And that charm was on full display the night he met Tanya, his future wife. I was throwing a '70s party and had rented a hall back in St. Albert. Mace—who was always a bit of a nudist for fun at parties—came out of the bathroom wearing nothing but a cowboy hat, cowboy boots and a makeshift thong that I had dared him to wear earlier in the night before we had some drinks. He rushed up on stage to join the band that was playing and, predictably, his thong underwear (which was hanging on by a thread anyway) somehow got twisted up, ripped off and tossed away. In front of about 200 people, Mace was naked on stage and rocking out to the music while doing butt clenches. Fortunately for him, Tanya was outside at the moment of his "naked romp"; by the time they were introduced to each other a little later that night, she had heard the buzz about his actions.

But for all his silliness and that wild unpredictable streak, Mace could also be a very serious and focused individual. After his professional hockey career concluded, he shocked all of us by going after a law degree at the University of Alberta. Most of us figured he had misunderstood what "passing the bar" actually meant. But with a lot of determination and dedication, Mace acquired that degree and was practicing law in Calgary in no time. He also settled down from those crazy-naked days, becoming a dedicated husband and father. And even while he matured, he never stopped being a loyal friend.

While this book is largely about the world of professional hockey and the experiences I witnessed and lived through, in a lot of ways it is also my lighthearted autobiography, and yet there is no way my story could be fully told without mentioning Mace everywhere in this book. I chose to give only a small glimpse of his life because, believe me, I could write another book entirely on what I call "the legend of Mace." To be honest, I wouldn't know where to begin. There was never a more loyal friend, husband and father than Dale Masson. I am not only proud and privileged to have been close to him for over 20 years, but not a day goes by that I don't think of him and remember how much of an influence he had on my life.

You are missed, my friend, but certainly not forgotten.

My earnings from this book will go directly to Mace's family—so that this might be a small help for Tanya and the boys, and a reminder of how truly special he was to all of us.

Index